Financing
the European
Community

CHATHAM HOUSE PAPERS

General Series Editor: William Wallace
West European Programme Director: Helen Wallace

The Royal Institute of International Affairs, at Chatham House in London, has provided an impartial forum for discussion and debate on current international issues for some 70 years. Its resident research fellows, specialized information resources, and range of publications, conferences, and meetings span the fields of international politics, economics, and security. The Institute is independent of government.

Chatham House Papers are short monographs on current policy problems which have been commissioned by the RIIA. In preparing the papers, authors are advised by a study group of experts convened by the RIIA, and publication of a paper indicates that the Institute regards it as an authoritative contribution to the public debate. The Institute does not, however, hold opinions of its own; the views expressed in this publication are the responsibility of the author.

CHATHAM HOUSE PAPERS

Financing the European Community

Michael Shackleton

The Royal Institute of International Affairs

Pinter Publishers
London

© Royal Institute of International Affairs, 1990

First published in Great Britain in 1990 by
Pinter Publishers Limited
25 Floral Street, London WC2E 9DS

Reprinted 1990

British Library Cataloguing in Publication Data

A CIP catalogue record for this book is available from the British Library

ISBN 0-86187-875-2 (Paperback)
0-86187-892-2 (Hardback)

Reproduced from copy supplied by
Stephen Austin and Sons Ltd
Printed and bound in Great Britain by
Biddles Ltd, Guildford and King's Lynn

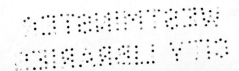

CONTENTS

To Jan, Katie and Lucy

ACKNOWLEDGMENTS

I should like to thank all those who helped towards the preparation of this paper. In London, the members of the Chatham House Study Group provided the ideal mixture of criticism and encouragement; my particular thanks go to Helen Wallace, the convener of the group. In the European Parliament, I benefited from discussions with many colleagues but I should especially like to mention Richard Corbett, François Vainker and Nick Hanley. Last but not least, Carolyn Wood, my secretary, ensured with the greatest calm and efficiency that the text was typed on time, despite my occasional interventions on the word processor.

All the faults that remain are attributable to the author alone and the views expressed are strictly personal.

December 1989   M.S.

1
INTRODUCTION

Has a new era of budgetary peace broken out in the European Community (EC)? There is no question that the European Council meeting held in Brussels in February 1988 marked the end of a long period of bitter argument about the financing of the EC and generated a widespread feeling that the Community had been dramatically reinvigorated. Whether this change in atmosphere will survive in the run-up to 1992 and thereafter is the central theme of this paper.

This introductory chapter is followed by five others. Chapter 2 outlines what was agreed at Brussels and in the months that followed, stressing its importance as compared with what had gone before. Chapter 3 points to the difficulties that are likely to arise as the Community seeks to fulfil the Brussels commitments. Chapter 4 discusses the problems involved in improving the quality as well as the volume of Community expenditure. Chapter 5 looks at the likely growth in pressure for the budget to accommodate new policy developments; and in Chapter 6, the whole budgetary debate is reviewed in terms of the contrast between collective and particular interests within the Community.

Characteristics of the budget
At the outset it is perhaps useful to include a brief reminder of the

1

principal characteristics of the Community budget. To assist in this review the reader will find in Annex I the contents of the financial provisions of the EEC Treaty (Articles 199 to 209). These provisions are central to Community financing but it is worth noting that they do not cover all of that activity. The rules governing the separate European Coal and Steel Community (ECSC) budget are somewhat different. In particular, the ECSC boasts the only example of a direct Community tax, imposing a levy on all coal and steel producers within the Community to help to finance its activities. There is also a considerable amount of borrowing and lending activity, managed both by the Commission and by the European Investment Bank (EIB), but in both cases these are separate operations which have not so far been incorporated within the budget. The European Development Fund (for the Lomé Convention aid to developing countries) also remains outside the budget at present.

Annex I provides a picture of what it is that distinguishes the Community budget both from national budgets and from the budgets of traditional international organizations and, in the process, why it has been the source of such contention over many years. Take, for example, Article 199 and its statement that: 'The revenue and expenditure shown in the budget shall be in balance'. This brings out a first and very important difference between the Community budget and national budgets which is that the Community budget cannot go into the red. Hence, there is no such thing as a Community debt and so none of the problems associated with financing national debts. On the other hand, extra revenue has to be found when expenditure exceeds the amount included in the budget.

A second feature of the Community budget is that it enjoys an important degree of autonomy: in this sense it differs markedly from traditional international organizations. This autonomy appears both in the nature of the revenue available to the Community and in the role played by Community institutions.

Although Article 200 of the Treaty still speaks of member states' contributions being determined on a set percentage basis, this is misleading in regard to the present situation. In 1970 a system of 'own resources' was established which was not based on such percentages. Rather, it provided for three kinds of revenue which are made available to the Community by the member states but which in legal terms belong to the Community. The three categories of resource are: first, customs levies and duties on products coming from outside the Community and subject to the Common Customs Tariff; second, agricultural levies on products coming from outside the Community; and third, a percentage of the VAT revenue collected in the member states, calculated by applying a uniform rate to the base used for assessing value added tax.

The introduction of this system meant that the Community was guaranteed revenue from the member states and no member state has been unwilling to make these resources available to it, in marked contrast, for example, to the United Nations, where default on payment is a regular occurrence. However, one characteristic of the system was that it made no attempt to reflect the relative economic strengths of the member states. Indeed, this combined with the character of Community spending to create the so-called British problem. Britain found itself contributing under the own resources system a much larger percentage of the total budget than it received in return in the form of Community spending. Its net contribution, i.e. the difference between own resources paid in and EC expenditure in Britain, came to exceed substantially that of any other member state with the exception of Germany. The attempt to rectify this situation dominated the Community agenda in the first years of the 1980s until the Fontainebleau Summit in 1984.

The Community institutions also enjoy considerable autonomy. Following the revision of the Treaty in 1975 the European Parliament (EP) acquired a significant role in the drawing-up of the Community budget. As Article 203, paragraphs 8 and 9, indicates, it has the power to reject the budget and to increase within defined limits the non-compulsory part of the budget described formally as 'expenditure other than that necessarily resulting from the Treaty or from acts adopted in accordance therewith'. The significance of this role in relation to non-compulsory expenditure can be seen by looking at Table 1, which shows the breakdown in 1989 between compulsory (CE) and non-compulsory (NCE) in the Commission's budget.

In global terms, NCE in payments represents close to 30% of the budget but this conceals major contrasts between the different

Table 1   Compulsory and non-compulsory expenditure:
Commission's appropriations for payments for 1989

Section	Non-compulsory expenditure (%)	Compulsory expenditure (%)
Staff and administration	86.79	13.21
EAGGF Guarantee Section	–	100.00
EAGGF Guidance Section	70.87	29.13
Fisheries	38.96	61.04
Regional development and transport	100.00	–
Social policy	100.00	–
Research, energy and technology	99.99	0.01
Development cooperation	74.68	25.32
Other	–	100.00
% of total appropriations	27.91	72.09
Total in ecus	12,312,691,586	31,791,486,930

Source: Commission of the European Communities (1989), *The Community Budget: The Facts in Figures*, p. 67.

areas of the budget. EAGGF Guarantee, for example, is made up of
CE to 100%. By contrast, the regional, transport and social sectors
are 100% NCE in character and nearly all the rest of the budget is
predominantly non-compulsory. The Parliament therefore has a
limited part to play in the budgetary procedure in relation to
agricultural guarantee expenditure (which represents 60% of the
total) but is allowed by Article 203(9) to have a much greater say as
to the level and distribution of other expenditure.

The Commission also has an important role. It has the sole duty
to implement the budget in accordance with Article 205 and is
responsible to the European Parliament alone for ensuring that the

Table 2   Growth of Community expenditure in relation to total of Member States' budgets and Community GDP (appropriations for payments)

Year	Expenditure (million ecu)	Growth in money terms (%)	Growth in real terms (%)[a]	Per capita expenditure Ecus	Per capita expenditure Growth in real terms with constant population (%)[b]	%of MSB[c]	%of GDP
1989	44,840.60	+2.33	-2.29[d]	138.29	+2.77[d]	3.69[e]	1.04[d]
1988	43,820.40	+21.16	+17.04	135.41	+16.59	3.56	1.09
1987	36,168.40	+2.83	-1.07	111.99	-2.23	3.14	0.98
1986	35,174.10	+23.71	+18.11	109.13	+16.86	3.08	0.99
1985	28,433.20	+4.35	-1.65	88.43	-2.86	2.70	0.92
1984	27,248.60	+8.73	+2.23	84.95	+1.06	2.90	0.98
1983	25,061.10	+13.99	+5.34	78.29	+4.31	2.70	0.96
1982	21,984.40	+19.26	+8.96	68.80	+7.33	2.50	0.86
1981	18,434.00	+13.91	+2.91	57.83	+1.41	2.40	0.81
1980	16,182.50	+12.01	-0.99	50.97	-2.84	2.70	0.80

Notes:
[a] Deflated by means of GDP (market prices) deflator.
[b] Deflated by means of GDP (market prices) deflator and rate of growth of Community population.
[c] MSB: Member States' budgets (Central government).
[d] Forecast.
[e] Estimate. Calculated by reference to Member States' public spending.

Source: Commission of the European Communities (1989), *The Community Budget: The Facts in Figures*, p. 14.

budget is implemented as voted. Similarly, Article 206a gives the Court of Auditors the job of ensuring that Community finance is properly used. These distinctive roles have generated constant tension between the Community institutions and member states over the limits of their respective powers. The Parliament in particular has constantly sought to assert its authority as a twin arm of the budgetary authority alongside the Council.

Figure 1 The growth of the Community budget, 1973–88

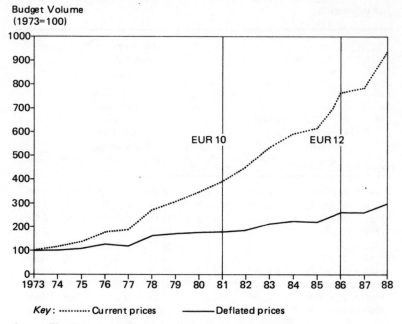

Budget Volume
(1973=100)

Key: ·········· Current prices ────── Deflated prices

Source: The Statistical Office of the European Parliament.

The third comment that should be made about the Community budget is that it is much bigger than the budget of other traditional international organizations but much smaller than national budgets. It is bigger than the budgets of other international organizations because in contrast to them, its operating expenditure is far greater than its administrative expenditure. At the same time, it is much smaller than national budgets because its role remains much more narrowly defined. It is not concerned, for example, with defence matters nor with issues such as social security which take up a very large fraction of national budgets. The net result, as Table 2 shows, is that despite a significant upward trend in the 1980s, the Community budget remains at under 4% of the total national budgets of the Twelve and around 1% of Community Gross Domestic Product.

However, the debate over the proper size of the budget is intense and there has been constant pressure, especially from within the

Table 3   The budgets of 1973 and 1988 compared (in ecus)

	1973	1988
EAGGF Guarantee	3,806,546,000	27,500,000,000
Repayments—old stocks	–	1,240,000,000
Monetary reserve	–	1,000,000,000
Other agriculture	–	69,406,000
Fisheries	–	281,046,000
Structural Funds		
— EAGGF Guidance	350,000,000	1,152,600,000
— European Social Fund	282,950,000	2,600,000,000
— European Regional Development Fund	–	2,980,000,000
Integrated Mediterranean Programmes and Portuguese industry programme	–	145,700,000
Other regional	–	4,600,000
Other social	–	171,667,100
Transport	–	71,110,000
Environment	–	32,909,500
Information and culture	–	40,700,000
Research and investment	74,686,830	915,675,000
Energy	–	111,140,000
Innovation and internal market	–	126,783,800
Development	48,177,000*	870,497,900
Administrative, operational and miscellaneous expenditure of all institutions	302,823,000	1,967,191,150**
Refunds to the Member States	260,467,841	2,534,370,074
Reserve		5,000,000
Total	5,134,493,871	43,820,396,524

Notes:
* food aid only.
**administrative expenditure only.

Community institutions, to increase its size and scope. Figure 1 indicates how it has increased in absolute terms since 1973 by a factor of around 9, and even in real terms around threefold.

What the figure does not show is the shape of the Community budget and the way it has evolved over the recent past. Table 3 compares the Community budget in 1973 and in 1988 and underlines the dramatic extension of Community activities in the last 15 years.

It can be noted, for example, that back in 1973 the European Regional Development Fund (ERDF) did not exist (it started in

7

1975) but now constitutes 7% of the total budget. There has also been a significant effort to expand expenditure into areas like transport and the environment. However, there has been one striking element of continuity. The guarantee section of the European Agricultural Guidance and Guarantee Fund (EAGGF), which is the centrepiece of the Common Agricultural Policy (CAP), continues to take up the largest proportion of the Community budget although the percentage has declined (from 75% to 61% between 1973 and 1988). All the other increases in spending over the 15-year period, however important in absolute terms as, for example, in development aid, have not kept pace with the dramatic growth in agricultural spending. Its tendency to expand has been the central budgetary question, with all efforts to limit the expansion proving fruitless up to now. The following chapters will consider whether 1988 marked a turning-point in this respect and will discuss the extent to which that year opened up a truly new debate on the shape of the Community budget.

2

SETTING THE SCENE

The crisis in which the Community found itself at the beginning of 1988 was unusually severe even by its own standards. For the first time the Council had been unable to meet the deadline laid down in Article 203(4) of the Treaty whereby it is obliged to adopt a draft budget by 5 October of the year preceding the financial year in question. The European Council meeting in Copenhagen in December 1987 had failed to come to a conclusion on the proposals presented by the Commission designed to combine increased resources with greater budgetary discipline. The whole financial structure of the Community looked to be in danger of collapse.

Within two months the situation was transformed. At an extraordinary session of the European Council in Brussels on 11/13 February, convened under the chairmanship of Chancellor Kohl of Germany, a whole series of major decisions were taken. These combined reinforced controls on expenditure, later incorporated in the decision on budgetary discipline (see Annex II), with a substantial increase in the volume of resources available to the EC. Remarkably the Heads of State and Government were prepared to look ahead to 1992 and to estimate the size of the budget in that year not simply in global terms but by category of expenditure. Subsequently, the Council, Commission and European Parliament went even further in the interinstitutional agreement (see Annex III) that

9

they signed in June 1988. This agreement includes a financial perspective with details for each of the years between 1988 and 1992.

The result was a dramatic change in the character of the budgetary procedure. Lord Plumb, then President of the EP, was able to sign the 1989 budget into law at the December 1988 plenary, the first time for four years that the budget had been approved without major controversy in advance of the financial year in question. By the beginning of 1989 Jacques Delors, President of the Commission, was able to claim in front of the EP that 'the Community is back under orderly management, that there is no more laxity or inconsistency'.

The financial crisis

To understand how this transformation came about, it is necessary to consider why the finances of the Community were in such difficulty. The nature of the crisis was primarily one of persistent resource scarcity. The revenue available to the Community had already begun to prove inadequate five years earlier when the 1% ceiling on the VAT call-up rate, which had been in force since 1970, was reached. In 1984 and 1985, extra funds were made available by intergovernmental agreements, pending the implementation of the decision taken at the Fontainebleau Summit in 1984 to increase the VAT ceiling to 1.4% from January 1986. This new limit was reached straightaway in 1986 and in 1987 the rate required would have been more like 1.9%, if it had not been for a number of essentially artificial devices for putting off expenditure. The most important of these was the delaying of the payment of agricultural advances under the EAGGF by two months. This saved or rather pushed forward indefinitely into the future about 4.5 billion ecus.

The reasons for this crisis were several, in part linked to the nature of the revenue system, in part a consequence of the difficulty of controlling expenditure. First, the own resources base was being eroded. On the one hand, the traditional 'own resources', customs duties and agricultural levies, were providing a constantly smaller percentage of revenue, as rates of duty went down and agricultural self-sufficiency was achieved in more and more products; on the other hand, VAT revenue (essentially a tax on consumption) was not expanding sufficiently to make up the difference, as consumption declined as a percentage of Community GDP. Moreover, the compensation mechanism agreed at Fontainebleau to remedy the British problem had the perverse effect of reducing the effective VAT call-up rate ceiling after 1986 from 1.4% to 1.25%. The cut in Britain's VAT contribution, amounting to two-thirds of the difference between its share of VAT payments and its percentage share of Community expenditure, was financed by an increase in the VAT contributions of the other member states up to a maximum of 1.4%, thereby bringing the uniform rate as applied to all member states down to 1.25%.

Second, the limits set by the budget proved insufficiently rigorous to prevent significant expansion in agricultural expenditure. The reasons for this are well known. As a paper from the Centre for European Policy Studies put it:

> The amounts entered into the budget for spending on agricultural support through the [EAGGF] Guarantee are forecasts of the amounts that are expected to be spent, not limitations on the amounts that can be spent. Actual spending on agricultural support will depend on decisions as to the prices set for agricultural products, but also on a range of external events which are beyond the control of the Community.[1]

Furthermore, the volume of agricultural stocks held in storage and the cost of that storage soared. In 1987 the Commission estimated that stock-related costs accounted for one-fifth of EAGGF Guarantee expenditure and that a 66% depreciation would be required to reduce the value of the stocks held to the prices that they could obtain on world markets.[2]

The Community had tried to tackle this problem. In December 1984 the Council laid down that the growth in agriculture expenditure should not exceed that of own resources. However, the existence of this rule made no difference to the level of expenditure: it only served as a yardstick by which the level of excess expenditure could be measured. This was most glaringly obvious in 1987 when the guideline was set at 22.9 billion ecus but real expenditure incurred in the course of the year was closer to 27 billion ecus. By then it was clear that something more drastic would have to be done, not least because some member states, including the United Kingdom, refused to contemplate any increase in resources without stricter control of expenditure.

The new agricultural guideline

What was agreed at Brussels in 1988 certainly marked a break with previous practice. A new agricultural guideline was established, namely that the annual growth rate of EAGGF Guarantee expenditure should not exceed 74% of the annual growth rate of Community GNP with as its starting-point a 1988 expenditure figure of 27.5 billion ecus (cf. Article 1 of Annex II). The character of this guideline was significantly different from that established in 1984. First, the Council of Ministers, when it converted the European Council's decisions into legislation, did not restrict itself to the 1984 formula of a set of conclusions. Instead, it adopted a decision binding on the member states, giving the new guideline a different legal status from its predecessor.

Second, the guideline was reinforced by a set of 'agricultural stabilizers'. Although their form differs from product to product, their basic intention is to provide a mechanism whereby the budget is not committed to ensuring an unlimited financial guarantee for agricultural production. For cereals, for example, a guarantee threshold was set (after bitter argument) at 160 million tons per annum. If production exceeds this figure, then producers are obliged to share in the effort to keep within budgetary limits by paying an extra co-responsiblity levy. Should the levy not raise sufficient revenue to ensure that the expenditure target is met, then the following year the intervention price or the minimum guaranteed by the Community is to be reduced by 3%.

Finally, the supervisory powers of the Commission in relation to agriculture were strengthened. In accordance with Article 6 of the budgetary discipline decision (see Annex II), it was invited to establish an 'early warning system', allowing it to trace the development of expenditure on a product-by-product basis and to compare actual expenditure with expenditure profiles based on monthly expenditure over the three preceding years. It now has the job of using its management powers to ensure expenditure does not exceed the forecast profile for the year. However, if it sees that these powers are not enough, then it has to invite the Council to strengthen the stabilizers already in operation. The Council, for its part, is obliged to act within two months to remedy the situation.

Increased resources

This set of controls on agricultural expenditure was matched by agreement on a new resource base which also represented a significant shift from the previous structure and one which corresponded closely to the approach of the Commission. It had suggested in COM(87)101 that the Community's revenue be linked directly to the economic fortunes of the Community as a whole. Its proposal was that for the period up to 1992, a limit of 1.4% of Community GNP be set on the level of revenue available under the own resources system. The idea was not, however, that the limit be exhausted over the next five years; rather it was suggested that there be gradual, annual rises up to 1.28% (in payments) in 1992, thus allowing considerable leeway for the unexpected as well as for the post-1992 era.

At the Brussels European Council, it was accepted that the overall ceiling on own resources be expressed in terms of the GNP of the Twelve but the percentage was set at 1.2% for payments and 1.3% for commitments up to 1992. In the own resources decision of 24 June 1988, intermediate, annual ceilings were also laid down for payments: 1.15% in 1988, 1.17% in 1989, 1.18% in 1990 and 1.19% in 1991.[3] This payments ceiling, it can be noted, relates only to own resources and does not therefore include other resources such as any surplus carried over from the previous year or the tax on the remuneration of Community officials. As the financial perspective linked to the interinstitutional agreement shows, the annual limits and overall limit were perceived as figures to be used only in exceptional circumstances. A margin for unforeseen expenditure of 0.03% was included in the perspective, depressing further the level of expenditure that could be authorized without 'a joint decision of the two arms of the budgetary authority, acting on a proposal from the Commission' (see Annex III, para. 12).

The importance of the agreement on increased resources reached at Brussels should not be underestimated. At a time of significant efforts to limit national budgets, it represented a commitment to allow the Community budget to expand over five years by as much as 14% in payments and 16.5% in commitments and this in real terms, at 1988 prices. In addition, the 1988 starting-point of 43.8 billion ecus was a high one, more than 7.5 billion ecus above the budget of the previous year, an absolute increase unparalleled in the history of the Community.

Nor was the difference between the conclusions of the European Council and the Commission proposals as great as it might seem. The Commission calculated the British rebate on the expenditure side and thus placed it within the GNP ceiling which it proposed. In the event, it was agreed to maintain the basic shape of the rebate as agreed at Fontainebleau and thereby to reduce the British revenue contribution while distributing the cost of the reduction among the other member states. Although the precise character of the rebate was modified to take account of the fact that the VAT assessment base was 'capped' and can no longer exceed 55% of the GNP of a member state, the important point was that it was *excluded* from the GNP limits agreed.[4] This, together with the fact that European Development Fund expenditure was maintained outside the Community budget, whereas the Commission had proposed to include it, took 0.11% GNP out of the expenditure side. It can thus even be argued that the European Council decision allowed for greater expenditure than the Commission had proposed.

Modification of resources

There was also agreement that the composition of the Community's resources should be modified. The Commission had made three main proposals: first, that the traditional own resources (customs duties and agricultural levies) be expanded by the inclusion of custom duties on products coming under the ECSC Treaty; second, that the maximum VAT call-up rate be reduced from 1.4% to 1% and be related to the actual, rather than the 'harmonized', VAT base;* and third, that a new resource should be created to supplement the existing sources of revenue. This 'fourth resource', as it came to be known, was to be calculated on the basis of the difference between the GNP and the VAT base of each Member State. It was thus designed to incorporate into the Community revenue system a measure of relative economic prosperity, given the tendency for consumption to take up a higher proportion of GNP in poorer states.

These proposals received a mixed response. The European Council agreed to incorporate ECSC duties, amounting to around 180 million ecus, into the revenue structure and it accepted the principle of creating a fourth resource. It did not, however, accept the shape for that resource proposed by the Commission. Already long before the Summit, in the summer of 1987, the member states had expressed their unanimous opposition to the use of the actual rather than a harmonized VAT base and the Commission had withdrawn this proposal, the only part of the 'Delors package' to be withdrawn in this way before the end of the negotiations. In Brussels, it was decided to amend the package further by maintaining the maximum call-up rate for VAT at 1.4% and by calculating the fourth resource in relation to the total volume of GNP, with the restriction referred to above, that the VAT base was only to be taken into account to the extent that it did not exceed 55% of GNP. The result was to reduce the contribution to own resources to be made by the fourth resource as well as making the system less progressive than it would otherwise have been.

However, the decision to establish a fourth resource was of greater significance than its precise shape. It meant that the Community disposed of a resource that, within the overall GNP limits, could expand and contract as necessary to balance budget revenue and expenditure. Its precise size would be determined by the gap left between agreed expenditure and the volume of revenue generated by all other sources of revenue. Thus, although the 1989 budget turned

---

* This refers to the EC device for calculating VAT payments precisely because the tax is not (yet) levied in a uniform way throughout the EC.

out to be 1 billion ecus larger than that of 1988, the contribution of the additional resource dropped from 7.1 billion ecus or 16.2% to 3.9 billion ecus or 8.7%. Such flexibility certainly has its advantages: it means, for example, that the British rebate no longer directly affects the volume of resources available to the Community in that the fourth resource is subject only to the overall GNP limits whereas a fixed ceiling applied and still applies to the VAT base. At the same time, the creation of such a resource seems likely to make it much more difficult to establish a more *communautaire* form of taxation.

Financial planning for 1992
The decisions taken at Brussels were not only remarkable in the impact that they had on the volume and the composition of Community revenue. It was also agreed that the revenue was to be used for particular purposes over the period 1988 to 1992. Chapter F of the Brussels conclusions, reproduced in Table 4, included estimates of expenditure for 1992 as well as the amounts sought in the 1988 budget, an act of medium-term financial planning not previously witnessed at any European Council meeting.

Subsequently, in the interinstitutional agreement these figures were revised to take account of the 1988 budget as adopted (in May) and expanded to include the intervening years as well as a break-down between compulsory and non-compulsory appropriations, the payments arising out of the commitments laid down and the GNP percentage involved.

Such precision was really very remarkable. In the past the Commission had duly observed the Council decision of 21 April 1970 concerning financial forecasts covering several years and had included each year in the preliminary draft budget 'a financial forecast for the three subsequent financial years'.[5] However, its significance was of limited importance as the Commission itself acknowledged when it put forward its proposals on future financing in February 1987:

Instead of remaining a simple forecasting exercise proposed by the Commission but virtually ignored by the budgetary

Table 4 Budget estimates for 1992 (commitments) in billion ecus (1988 prices)

	1988	1992
EAGGF Guarantee Section	27.5	29.6
Financing of destocking measures	1.2	1.4
Set-aside—aids to income	–	0.6
Structural Funds	7.7	12.9
EPIDP (European Programme for Industrial Development in Portugal)	0.1	0.1
Total of structural actions	7.8	13.0
Policies with multiannual allocations (Research—Integrated Mediterranean Programmes)	1.4	2.4
Other policies	1.7	2.8
Reimbursements and administration	3.5	2.0
Monetary reserve	1.0	1.0
Total	44.1	52.8

authority, these multiannual forecasts would become an instrument for the medium-term planning of Community finances.[6]

One reason why the Commission was able to turn its new ideas into a realistic prospect was that it set the multiannual forecasts firmly in the framework of budgetary discipline. At the centre of the Commission's ideas was the notion that the Community could hope to win a higher volume of resources only if the member states were convinced that those resources were controlled more closely than in the past. Thus it argued that increased resources giving 'budget security' had to

be accompanied by tighter budget discipline and greater stringency in the establishment and execution of the budget. The proposals for a higher resources ceiling and those for tougher discipline arrangements and greater strictness of management then constitute an indivisible whole.[7]

Thus, Chapter F of the European Council's conclusions and the detailed figures found in the interinstitutional agreement have to be understood as providing the member states with a clear yardstick against which the development of expenditure can be measured as well as offering an important level of budget security to the Community.

In this process, the European Council also paved the way for a reduction of institutional conflict within the Community by inviting the Council to 'aim to agree with the European Parliament an understanding on the implementation of the Decisions of the European Council covering the whole period up to 1992'.[8] The German Presidency of the Council subsequently made strenuous efforts to convert this undertaking into a formal text and negotiations with the Commission and Parliament were successfully completed four months later.

The signing of the interinstitutional agreement meant that both arms of the budgetary authority, the Council and the European Parliament, were committed to the objectives established at Brussels. Moreover, those objectives could not be modified by one party without the consent of the other, as Article 4 of the agreement indicates. This was not something that was easy for all delegations in the Council to accept as it meant that the EP was being given a right of veto in relation to increases in EAGGF Guarantee expenditure beyond the guideline. However, it could also be seen as offering an additional guarantee against the guideline being breached. Any upward revision of the guideline requires not only a qualified majority in the Council but also the agreement of the Parliament, acting by a majority of its members and three-fifths of the votes cast, in accordance with the provisions of Article 203(9) of the Treaty.

The EP itself saw in the agreement not only a reinforcement of its role in relation to all expenditure but also a guarantee of substantial increases in areas of non-compulsory expenditure (NCE), such as the structural funds and research which it had advocated over many years. In particular, these increases would not be subject to the vagaries of agricultural expenditure. Article 8 of the agreement includes an express undertaking that 'any revision of the compulsory expenditure given in the financial perspective will not cause the amount of non-compulsory expenditure shown in the perspective to be reduced'.

Why this should be important to the Parliament can be understood only in the context of what had happened previously. In December 1984, the Council made it clear that in future it intended to maintain the increase in non-compulsory expenditure to the maximum rate determined by economic indicators, as laid down in Article 203(9) of the Treaty. In 1986, this proved impossible, given the accession of Spain and Portugal, but in the case of the 1987 budget its refusal to contemplate an increase partly explained why the budget had not been approved by the end of the previous year. In February 1987, agreement was eventually reached between the European Parliament and the Council on the basis of an increase of 8.149%. The Parliament argued that the Council had agreed to exceed the maximum rate of 8.1% and the Council retorted that the maximum rate was only determined to one decimal point. However, the real lesson was that the room for manoeuvre in the non-compulsory sector was almost non-existent at a time when agricultural expenditure was constantly exceeding the guideline established.

Moreover, the Commission indicated in COM(87)101 that the scope for increases in NCE was likely to decrease sharply in the period up to 1992. Between 1980 and 1984 the maximum rate had never fallen below 10%: it had varied between 11.6% and 14.5%. In 1987 it had dropped to 8.1% and the Commission anticipated that this trend would continue with the figure dropping below 5% in 1989 and staying at that level until 1992, under the impact of substantially reduced inflation rates. That would mean that in real terms, NCE expenditure would not increase by more than 2% in any year between 1988 and 1992. Although in the event the rates were a little higher than expected – 7.4% in 1988, 5.8% in 1989 and 6.1% in 1990 – the main contention of the Commission that NCE would be under severe pressure with the existing maximum rates proved correct.

The Commission considered that such a situation was not tenable in view of the commitments that the Community had entered into by agreeing the Single European Act (SEA). Thus, it was prepared to

19

put a price on the strengthening of economic and social cohesion, arguing for a doubling of expenditure in real terms on the structural funds. Few, however, thought the richer member states would be prepared to pay such a high price. Nothing that happened prior to the Brussels meeting suggested that the poorer states could hope for anything close to a doubling. And yet at the meeting it was agreed to double the real volume of the structural funds by 1993 as compared with 1987. This meant an increase from 7,233 million ecus in 1987 (as expressed in 1988 prices) to 14,500 million ecus (again in 1988 prices), six years later. To enable this goal to be achieved, the conclusions of the European Council specified that the resources entered in the budget for 1988 (7,700 million ecus in commitments) be increased each year thereafter by 1,300 million ecus so as to reach a total of 12,900 million ecus (1988 prices) in 1992.[9] To achieve a doubling by 1993, the final year will need to see an even bigger jump of 1,600 million ecus.

A new kind of expenditure
The amount of money involved was not the only remarkable feature of the decision to double the size of the funds. It also effectively created a new kind of Community expenditure which might be termed 'compulsory non-compulsory'. Although structural spending remains in the non-compulsory sector, it is no longer subject to the vagaries of the budgetary procedure. The annual increase of 1,300 million ecus is guaranteed in advance of the debate on the budget: it represents both a legal ceiling to be respected and a political target to be attained. Indeed this makes it in one sense more binding than compulsory expenditure (CE). Although CE is designed to cover the areas where the Community has financial obligations towards individuals within the EC or other states outside it, it is not considered a target to be attained. If, for example, agricultural appropriations are not required because of a rise in the value of the dollar, then the appropriations are simply not used. By contrast, the Brussels decisions created an expectation that the increases in structural spending would not only be entered in the budget but also spent. Otherwise, the commitment to double the

funds would be of little value. As we shall see, this poses important problems in relation to the utilization of appropriations.

The creation of a new kind of expenditure in this way posed an interesting problem in relation to the Parliament. The major increase in structural spending could not take place without the maximum rate provisions being exceeded. However, Article 203 of the Treaty gives the Parliament important rights in relation to NCE: it is entitled to increase the draft budget adopted by the Council by half the maximum rate and to have the last word on the allocation of expenditure within the non-compulsory sector. In other words, the EP could not be bound to accept the decisions of the European Council on increases in structural spending nor prevented from using a fraction of that increase for other areas of policy. The European Council did attempt to address this problem by creating a distinction between 'privileged' and 'non-privileged' NCE, the former reserved for those policies subject to multiannual financing decisions for the period up to 1992 (structural funds, IMPs and research). Whereas the privileged sector (located in categories 2 and 3 of the financial perspective) could rise by the rates corresponding to the figures in Chapter F of the European Council's conclusions, the non-privileged (concentrated in Category 4 of the perspective) could only increase in accordance with the maximum rate. This distinction was strongly contested by the Parliament. It argued that there was no basis for it in the Treaties and feared that it would lead to a dilution of its budgetary powers. At the same time, it had strongly campaigned for the increase in the funds and wished to see this secured.

The significance of the difficulty was substantially diminished by the interinstitutional agreement, which gave the Parliament important guarantees as to the evolution of all NCE over the period up to 1992. In particular, paragraph 15 ensured that the major battles over the level of the maximum rate that had raged in earlier years need not recur:

The two arms of the budgetary authority agree to accept, for the financial years 1988 to 1992, the maximum rates of increase

21

for non-compulsory expenditure deriving from the budgets
established within the ceilings set by the financial perspective.

This phrase did not eliminate all scope for disagreement but it did set
relations between the two institutions on a different footing at least
for the time being.

As the arguments between the Council and the Parliament over
the expansion of non-agricultural expenditure as well as the control
of the CAP had been at the centre of budgetary debate for so long, it
was perhaps natural to assume that the budget would now become a
less important issue. If all the Community institutions, including the
EP, were prepared to accept an expenditure framework for the years
up to 1992, why should it not be possible for the centre of debate to
pass to other areas? The remainder of this paper will seek to show
why this question misses the point. The problem of acute resource
scarcity may indeed have been resolved for the time being but this
will only serve to push the budgetary debate into new areas. Between
now and 1992 there are certain to be some budgetary surprises and
indeed to assume otherwise is to misunderstand the character of the
Community.

3
FULFILLING THE BRUSSELS COMMITMENTS

The first question raised by the Brussels settlement is whether or not it will be possible to fulfil the commitments entered into. The fact that the appropriations are guaranteed does not of itself ensure that policy objectives will be achieved. This relationship between what is entered in the budget and the Community's objectives has always been a vexed one. On the one hand, in relation to compulsory expenditure and in particular EAGGF Guarantee expenditure, agreed legislation has determined the amount actually spent; on the other hand, in the case of non-compulsory expenditure it has often been difficult to make use of the money included in the budget. In the former case, the philosophy of the *guichet ouvert* has prevailed; in the latter, there has always been a time-consuming and uncertain process of negotiated allocation involving the Commission and the member states. In one sense, the Brussels European Council sought to soften the differences between the two approaches: it insisted that the guarantees of the CAP no longer be automatic and it called for a doubling of spending on the structural funds to be ensured.

The distinction between the various types of expenditure was further blurred by placing all expenditure together in the financial perspective. The result is a degree of ambiguity as to the status of the figures found there. In particular, are they to be considered expenditure targets as well as ceilings on expenditure? In the draft budget for 1989, for example, the Council stated its view that 'the amounts in the financial perspective constitute ceilings which may not be exceeded, but which may be attained'.[1] As a result it did not enter the total amount available for EAGGF Guarantee or for other policies under category 4 of the financial perspective, but on the other hand it went very close to exhausting the total for structural measures (category 2). The Parliament, for its part, decided to enter appropriations up to the figures available under the perspective for the non-compulsory categories, in particular category 4, while sharing the restrictive attitude of the Council towards category 1 (EAGGF Guarantee expenditure). Thus, neither arm of the budgetary authority considers that all the categories of expenditure in the financial perspective are to be exhausted but they disagree as to where targets for expenditure and ceilings on expenditure should converge.

This disagreement means that there will be some dispute as to whether the commitments made at Brussels have been met or not. Neither Council nor Parliament will insist on exhausting category 1 and both will view success in terms of not exceeding the guideline, but the Council alone will not be seeking to exhaust category 4. However, the creation of an intermediate category in the shape of privileged non-compulsory expenditure is likely to make the range of argument more limited. Here the discussion will be restricted to the two main areas on which agreement was reached at Brussels, namely agriculture and the structural funds.

Agriculture

As far as agriculture is concerned, the whole nature of the debate was changed dramatically in the course of 1988 because the strengthening of the dollar and drought in the United States combined to push world prices upwards and thereby to reduce demands on the Community budget. The result was that the Commission introduced a rectifying letter in the course of the 1989 budgetary procedure and the level of agricultural appropriations for 1989 was reduced by over 1 billion ecus. Subsequently, the Commission estimated the requirements for 1990 at 26,858 million ecus or nearly 3.8 billion ecus below the guideline figure established on the basis of the Brussels decisions.

Figure 2   Agricultural stocks (1984–8)

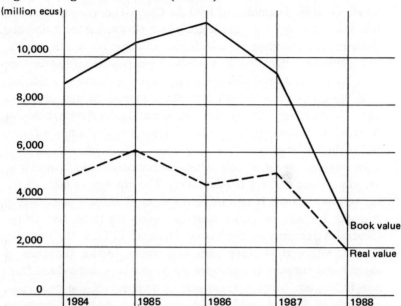

Source: Commission of the European Communities (1989), *The Community Budget: The Facts in Figures*, p. 43.

At the same time, it calculated that the stock situation could return to normal by the end of 1990 or two years earlier than envisaged in February 1988.[2] As Figure 2 indicates, there was a dramatic reduction in 1988 not only in the real and book values of agricultural stocks but also in the difference between the two values. In this way the decisions taken in Brussels to depreciate the value of existing and new stocks (cf. Annex II, Article 4) combined with external factors to reduce dramatically the pressure on the agricultural budget.

The availability of a substantial volume of unused appropriations within the agricultural guideline did not lead to major increases in annual price levels when agriculture ministers met in the spring of 1988 and 1989. It did, however, encourage calls for allocating part of the 'surplus' for extra support in the agricultural sector. At the end of 1988, for example, the European Parliament called for the addition of 200 million ecus to the agricultural budget to weaken the impact of the co-responsibility levy in the cereals sector on small

25

producers and to reinforce direct income aids to small farmers. Similarly, at the beginning of 1989 the Council adopted measures in reforming the beef and veal sector which eliminated the automatic element in intervention but which also involved an overall increase in expenditure which would not have been possible if expenditure were already at a level corresponding to the agricultural guideline. And there was even discussion in the Commission that the move away from the advances system (introduced under duress) could be reversed, with the member states being paid once again in advance rather than in arrears.

However, it would be rash to jump to premature conclusions over the importance of these developments. The pressure to limit spending remains strong. It cannot be forgotten that the Community is engaged in international negotiations within the framework of the General Agreement on Tariffs and Trade (GATT), in the Uruguay Round, where it is being pressed hard to reduce its levels of agricultural support and to open up its markets to products from non-EC states. Moreover, no one is unaware of the precarious character of the favourable new circumstances. As the Commission pointed out, 'the depreciation of stocks as soon as they are formed leaves the budget fully exposed to the ups and downs of production'.[3] In more general terms, the Community budget remains vulnerable to external circumstances, whose direction cannot confidently be predicted. They could just as well take an unfavourable direction before 1992 as they have taken a favourable one in 1988 and 1989. It is worthwhile recalling that the dollar rose steadily in value against the ecu between 1981 and 1985 from 0.895 ecu to 1.310 ecu before dropping to 1.02 ecu in 1986 and as low as 0.80 ecu the following year. Every cent drop was reckoned to cost the Community around 100 million ecus.

The likelihood that the agricultural guideline would be breached quickly was reduced by the fact that the Brussels European Council took a very generous base from which to calculate future estimates of EAGGF expenditure. It accepted a figure of 27.5 billion ecus as the amount to be allocated to expenditure in 1988 and from which the guideline for subsequent years was to be assessed. This represented an increase of expenditure from 1987 to 1988 of 4.6 billion ecus or 10% of the total 1988 budget. Subsequently when the 1989 budget was revised downwards and EAGGF Guarantee expenditure was reduced to 26.8 billion ecus, this was still 3.8 billion ecus or 16.5% above the 1987 figure.

Moreover, the guideline agreed in Brussels does not apply to as wide a definition of agricultural expenditure as the Commission had wished. It had argued that the guideline should include *all* costs connected with the disposal and depreciation of stocks. However, although it was agreed in Brussels that stock depreciation become a legal obligation rather than remaining discretionary, it was decided that a distinction should be made between existing stocks and new stocks, with the former being excluded from the guideline. The amounts involved for the depreciation of existing stocks (1.2 billion ecus in 1988 and 1.4 billion ecus in each of the four subsequent years) are thus to be entered each year under Title 8 of the budget (Repayments and aid to Member States, Loan Guarantees and Miscellaneous) rather than Titles 1 and 2, where EAGGF Guarantee expenditure is otherwise concentrated.

Nor was this the only way in which EAGGF Guarantee expenditure was defined generously. In Brussels it was also decided to establish outside the guideline a monetary reserve of 1000 million ecus to cover 'developments caused by significant and unforeseen movements in the dollar/ecu market rate compared to the dollar/ecu rate used in the budget' (see Annex II, Article 10). The nature of this reserve is highly unorthodox from a budgetary point of view. Although the amount is entered in the budget, it is not, unlike all other appropriations, to be called up from the member states and put to use, unless the dollar falls in value and then only if the additional costs go above 400 million ecus. It should also be pointed out that the flow of appropriations can go in the opposite direction, again only if the savings top 400 million ecus. In this case, the appropriations are to be transferred from the operational lines of the budget to the reserve, the amount remaining at the end of the year being cancelled and thus contributing to a budgetary surplus. This is what happened in the second half of 1989, when the Commission proposed that 819 million ecus be transferred to the reserve, as agricultural expenditure during the year had turned out to be that much lower than expected.

The effect of these exceptions to the guideline is that the true volume of agricultural appropriations is somewhat concealed. If both the depreciation of existing stocks and the monetary reserve are added to the EAGGF Guarantee figure, then the total represents 68% of the total 1988 budget (as expressed in payments) declining to 63% of the total in 1992 as envisaged in the financial perspective. This represents a substantial retreat from the position taken by the Commission in COM(87)101 where it foresaw agricultural guarantee expenditure amounting to only 55% of the budget in 1992.

With such a generous starting-point it would indeed have been astonishing if the guideline laid down had already been under pressure. However, the question that has to be asked is what would happen if that guideline came under pressure. The new system of agricultural stabilizers and the 'early warning system' will certainly make it possible to tell in advance where problems are likely to occur. Such knowledge existed before but it did not extend far beyond the Commission and certainly was not systematically integrated into the policy process. In future, demands for action, not least from the European Parliament, will be heard at a much earlier stage and with more information to back them up.

It remains to be seen whether this greater transparency will make it easier for agriculture ministers to reach decisions in the Council. In relation to the debate on the Commission's price proposals for the next marketing year, it has been agreed that 'if the Commission considers that the outcome of the Council's discussions on these price proposals is likely to exceed the costs put forward in its original proposal, the final decision shall be referred to a special meeting of the Council' (see Annex II, Article 5). As the Brussels conclusions made clear, this special meeting is to be attended both by the ministers of finance and by the ministers of agriculture and it will have the sole power to adopt a decision. A compulsory conclave cannot guarantee that a way will not be found to exceed the guideline but it does reduce the scope for excuses, through institutionalizing the notion of collective responsibility in Council decision-making.

On the other hand, for the detailed operation of the agricultural markets, no such joint meeting is foreseen in the event of the Agriculture Council not meeting the two-month deadline within which it is expected to act in response to Commission proposals to strengthen the stabilizers. Under such circumstances it is the Commission which would be faced with very important decisions about the payments it would make to member states. To understand why, it is necessary to say a little about the way CAP financing has been modified.

Changes in the advances system

At the Brussels European Council, it was agreed to establish on a continuing basis the temporary change in the financing of the CAP agreed at a previous European Council in Brussels in June 1987. Under this change, instead of the Community advancing EAGGF Guarantee expenditure to the member states *before* the payments are made to producers, the Commission now makes the appropriations available to the member states *after* they have declared that they have made the payments. A number of member states were very reluctant to acknowledge the importance of this change and thus insisted that the Community system still be referred to in terms of 'advances' (albeit delayed) rather than 'reimbursements'. Moreover, the advances are still paid on a global basis and not chapter-by-chapter or product-by-product.

However, the change has altered the character of the advances system in two significant ways. First, it has made it possible for the Commission to oblige the member states to provide information justifying Community payment, rather than assuming it will be made available without question. Moreover, member states now have to give this information 'for each common market organization' (i.e. each product), thus weakening the global character of the advances system (see Annex II, Article 7). In practical terms the Commission has already agreed a system with the member states, whereby a telex is sent by the member states by the 10th of the month following that in which the producers were paid, indicating amounts by chapter. The Commission then has to pay the 'advance' by the 3rd of the next month, unless the telex is delayed. This may not allow time to check in detail whether payment is justified

29

but it nevertheless makes the member states subject to a more rigorous regime than that which existed previously.

The second change in the advances system was hinted at by the Commission in the declaration it made at the Brussels European Council. It declared that not only did prudent management require that member states provide adequate information before payment was made but also that payment was only possible 'to the extent that, as under the budgetary procedure for other compulsory expenditure, the availability of credits is established by chapter, i.e. by common market organization'.[4] Admittedly it goes on to say that where credits are not available it will propose transfers, but the question then is what if there is no possibility of transfers or if the transfers are not agreed to by the budgetary authority?

It is here that we return to the question of what happens if the Council cannot decide to strengthen the agricultural stabilizers. One answer would be that the Commission would simply stop paying the part of the global advances relative to the product in question. It would know that the producers were still being paid from national funds but could refuse repayment until the legislation was modified. This is, however, a move which would be highly controversial in legal and institutional terms.

Within the Community, there has been a constant tension between those, on one side, who have argued that Community law as expressed in legislation should take precedence over that law as expressed through the budget and those, on the other, who have maintained the converse. The Council of Ministers has traditionally taken the first view, as it is well aware that it has the final say in legislative matters but not on all parts of the budget; in contrast, the European Parliament has been the champion of the second view, wishing to take full advantage of its prominent role in the budgetary procedure and aware of the way that the character of existing legislation has been at the root of agricultural expenditure exceeding budgetary provisions. The Parliament won a notable victory in this debate in June 1988 when the budgetary discipline decision was due to be adopted. A delegation from the Parliament met with the Council in accordance with the conciliation procedure whereby the two parties can seek to reconcile their positions on legislative acts which have far-reaching financial implications. In this case, the Council was persuaded to include in the text the following article, expressly linking legislative decisions to the availability of finance:

> The financial implementation of any Council Decision exceeding the budget appropriations available in the general budget or the appropriations provided for in the financial estimates may not take place until the budget and, where appropriate, the financial estimates have been suitably amended according to the procedure laid down for each of these cases (Annex II, Article 16).

There remains the question of whether the Commission would be prepared to carry through the logical consequence of this text if the Council refused to strengthen the stabilizers sufficiently. And what of the member states who have normally sought to put legislation beyond the reach of budgetary law? How many member states would be willing to accept such action from the Commission without demur? Their difficulty would be that the alternative would cause the agricultural budget to overrun, thus undermining the Brussels accord.

The structural funds

The attempt to render agricultural expenditure less automatic than hitherto went along with a commitment to increase non-compulsory spending and notably to double the structural funds by 1993. It was recognized that this could not happen without the maximum rate being exceeded. Hence, the creation of the distinction referred to earlier between 'privileged' and 'non-privileged' NCE. However dubious in legal terms it may be, it clearly reflected the political priorities fixed by the member states for the next five years. Their attitude was strikingly underlined in the course of the 1989 budgetary procedure, when the Council incorporated in its draft the precise amounts proposed by the Commission for the structural funds (with a small exception of 20 million ecus in payments for the Social Fund) but made the traditional reductions in other areas of non-compulsory spending such as development aid. The rules of the budgetary game had clearly changed.

What, though, is going to be of considerable interest is whether the priorities set by the European Council can be followed when it comes to the implementation of expenditure. A first reason for raising this point is that the rules governing the use of appropriations were modified following the Brussels European Council. Under Article 202 of the EEC Treaty, 'any appropriations, other than those relating to staff expenditure, that are unexpended at the end of the financial year may be carried forward to the next financial year only'. On this basis all differentiated appropriations, designed to finance multiannual programmes such as the structural funds, research and the Integrated Mediterranean Programmes (IMPs), had hitherto had an effective life of two years. If they were not used up by the end of the year for which they were included in the budget, they were automatically carried over for a second year. Hence the available appropriations in any given year were consistently higher than those found in the budget. Only if appropriations were not used up in their second year were they cancelled.

However, Council Regulation 2049/88 introduced a much stricter interpretation of the Treaty provisions. Automatic carryovers can no longer take place; instead, differentiated appropriations (i.e. those relating to multiannual programmes) not used 'at the end of the financial year for which they were entered shall, as a rule, lapse'. Some exceptions are provided for, such as when the Council adopts legislation under which expenditure can be authorized, towards the end of the financial year. However, their coverage is very limited: at the beginning of 1989, the first year of application of the new rules, only 15.9 million ecus in commitments and 48.1 million ecus in payments were carried over. In general terms, one can say that the vast bulk of appropriations will have to be used in the year for which they were included in the budget.

This is of considerable importance for the areas in which major expansion is anticipated, given that utilization rates of appropriations outside EAGGF Guarantee have been a regular source of concern in the past. In 1987, even including EAGGF appropriations, the overall level of utilization amounted to 96.7% in commitments and only 94.3% in payments.[5] Unless this pattern can be improved, it will be very difficult to bring about an effective, rather than a theoretical, doubling of the funds. Given the size of the increases envisaged, even a small percentage of unused appropriations would have a significant impact. If, for example, 5% of the structural fund appropriations were not committed in 1989, this would represent some 460 million ecus which would be 'lost' and the equivalent amount in 1992 would be over 700 million ecus. Over the four-year period from 1989 to 1992 the loss would cumulate to close on 2.5 billion ecus, or more than is available for all expenditure commitments on other policies under category 4 of the financial perspective in 1989.

It was in response to this possibility that the interinstitutional agreement envisages unspent appropriations being added to the appropriations of a subsequent year. Paragraph 11 states that 'if the allocations provided in the financial perspective for multiannual programmes cannot be used in full during a given year, the institutions party to the Agreement undertake to authorize the transfer of the remaining allocations'. As Nicoll (1988) indicates, the word 'transfer' (in French, *transfert*) is a new one in the Community's budgetary vocabulary.[6] It is not to be confused with the transfers or *virements*, made in the course of a year between budgetary chapters, nor is it equivalent to the idea of carryovers or *reports*.

As a result, the mechanism for the implementation of such a transfer is anything but clear. It would appear to require that the amount unspent be added to the budget of year N + 1 by means of a supplementary budget, which would incorporate a positive balance from the year N. However, if such a balance did not exist, the Commission would have to propose a revision of the financial perspective, for example, through application of the margin for unforeseen circumstances of 0.03% of GNP. This margin amounts to well over 1 billion ecus and might therefore be considered to be more than sufficient. However, what would happen if more than one area of expenditure were bidding for a portion of the 0.03%? Or alternatively what if the backlog accumulated over more than one year in a single area, such as the structural funds, exceeded the funds available? To these questions the agreement itself can give no answer.

A second reason for questioning the fulfilment of the ambition of the European Council can be sought in the decision-making structures both within and outside the Community institutions. When automatic carryovers were abolished, this was seen by some as providing a mechanism for making the spending departments in the Commission more efficient and less inclined to linger over decisions. However, it is by no means certain that this will be the result. Instead, the effect may be to encourage spending without due consideration simply because the effect of not doing so is that the appropriations will be lost and can only be recovered by a very complex procedure.

Moreover, it is still not certain that the Commission will have enough staff of the right kind to process applications. In the course of the 1988 budget procedure it asked for an extra 435 posts, most of them to deal with the impact of the doubling of the structural funds. Of these, 217 were granted and so the Commission requested the remainder for 1989: these were finally granted by the budgetary authority in February 1989. However, these posts have to be distributed over a number of different services. Take, for example, the Directorate General for Regional Policy (DG XVI). In 1986 it had 54 administrative staff, a figure which had risen to 82 by the spring of 1989. A 50% increase in three years may sound large but the staff remains a very small number to cope with the very substantial increase in funds now available. It is true that the move from projects to programmes in the area of the funds will reduce the sheer volume of applications, but the task will not become any easier, as we shall see below.

However, even if the Commission staff are able to adapt in time, there is a further imponderable and that is the attitude of the member states. Will they be able to come forward with a sufficient number of proposals of adequate quality? The portents are not altogether favourable. One can recall that in the European Social Fund, at the beginning of 1986, over 20% of all the commitments entered into since 1970 were still outstanding. Despite enquiries by the Commission, only just over half of the backlog was cleared by means of payment, the remainder, amounting to 1.3 billion ecus, being cancelled or used elsewhere. It is hard not to infer that member states were not unduly concerned that they had submitted projects which proved to be unsuccessful.

Moreover, the experience of the IMPs has shown how difficult it is, even when member states are eager to benefit, for programmes to be prepared with the requisite speed. Although the IMPs were given a place in the budget from 1983 it was a constant struggle to use the appropriations. After two years of preparatory work, in 1985 a substantial figure of 140 million ecus in commitments was entered but less than 5% of them were used. The following year the commitments available rose to over 360 million ecus and payments were set at over 140 million ecus. Again, though, the utilization rates were dramatically low, only just exceeding 10%. Finally, in 1987, the utilization rates for both commitments and payments rose markedly to 53.5% and 60% respectively. Only now can it be said that programmes and appropriations are starting to coincide.

There are, however, some reasons for supposing that these past difficulties will not be as prominent in future. First, the rules governing the use of appropriations have been amended so that commitments are only valid for a set period. In future, the legal commitments entered for measures extending over more than one financial year shall contain a time limit for implementation which must be specified to the recipient in due form when the aid is granted.[7] This limit can be modified by the Commission 'in special circumstances', but it seems unlikely that the Community will in future be faced with the problem of the accumulation of commitments from earlier years on a scale comparable with that which existed in 1986/7.

Secondly, the new regulations allow for substantial levels of advances. A first advance of up to 50% can be supplemented by a second one taking the total up to 80% provided that 'at least half of the first advance has been used and that the operation is progressing at a satisfactory rate and in accordance with the objectives laid down'.[8] Although a similar rate of advances was possible, for example, under the 1984 ERDF regulation, the difference is that the advances now apply to overall plans rather than specific projects. A part of a plan may now be subject to delay without thereby endangering the payment of the advance, whereas in the past difficulties with a particular project necessarily meant that the maximum advance could not be paid.

It is still too soon to judge whether this more optimistic assessment will be vindicated. What one can say is that the major increases in the non-agricultural sector have raised expectations, particularly in the poorer member states. Failure to implement them effectively will raise questions as to the genuineness of the Community's commitment to the goal of economic and social cohesion as enshrined in the Single European Act. However, the very existence of this commitment may tempt the Community institutions to put more emphasis on guaranteeing that the appropriations are spent than on ensuring they are spent wisely. Similarly, in the agricultural sector too much attention devoted to ensuring the containment of expenditure will cloud debate on the use and misuse of the appropriations that are available. Hence the importance of ensuring that the question of value for money does not slip off the agenda in the coming years.

4
GETTING VALUE FOR MONEY

The discussion so far has concentrated on whether or not the Community is able either to curtail expenditure or to meet the expenditure targets it has set itself. In neither case has the question been asked: is this the best way of using the money that is available to the Community? Are the Community's citizens getting value for money? Indeed these are questions which have arguably never been to the forefront of the Community agenda. There has been a tendency to argue that monies are well spent provided that they are spent in accordance with the legal criteria laid down in the authorizing regulations. Broader criteria of cost-effectiveness have been applied only intermittently. Now, in the light of the decisions taken in Brussels, the need to examine the justification for expenditure is being looked at afresh.[1]

The issue will be considered here under two headings: first, the question of fraud in the agricultural sector and second, the way in which the increased appropriations available for economic and social cohesion are used. In both cases it will be argued that better value for money cannot simply be willed by the Council but requires a recognition of the need to develop the way the Community institutions operate. There is no shortcut, no painless path to increased effectiveness.

Agricultural fraud

It was suggested earlier that the change in the advances system of EAGGF financing meant that the Commission was rather better able to manage the requests for payment from the member states. However, it would be foolish to assume that such controls can go much beyond checking whether the expenditure has been disbursed in accordance with the correct regulations. The Commission cannot hope to be able to see whether wider criteria have been met.

This issue came very much to the fore in the first part of 1989 following the publication of the Annual Report of the Court of Auditors on the 1987 budget year, which sought to go beyond generalities about the level of fraud in the Community by concentrating on the detailed working of the agricultural markets.[2] The Court of Auditors made a special study of the export refunds paid to Community exporters of certain agricultural products to enable them to compete in third-country markets where prices are generally below those within the Community. It recalled that in 1987 these refunds constituted over 9 billion ecus or around 41% of the total expenditure on EAGGF Guarantee. It concentrated its attention on the beefmeat sector and carried out investigations in four member states, Britain, Ireland, France and Germany, which together account for 80% of the expenditure in this sector.

The findings of the Court in relation to the controls applied for export refunds are extremely critical of the practices found. It noted cases where claims for refunds were granted even though the product was not exported at all, the product exported was not beef and the product was not exported to the destination intended. The Court concluded that 'the scope and quality of national controls over the payment of export refunds, particularly in the beef sector, do not give a reasonable assurance that the expenditure concerned was legally and regularly incurred'.[3]

Subsequently, the Select Committee on the European Communities of the House of Lords in the UK produced a report which was equally critical of the weaknesses in the existing system of controls, with particular reference to the United Kingdom.[4] It noted, for example, that the (British) National Audit Office declared that it 'has no responsibility for, and does not organize its work to provide, the audit of Community operations'. It pointed to the lack of lucid and compatible instructions as to the checks to be carried out by the national authorities. It concluded by condemning the sums lost as a public scandal, striking at the very roots of democratic societies.

Both the Council and the Commission considered it essential to respond to these criticisms. The Council responded initially in the context of the discussion on the discharge to the Commission, the procedure whereby the actual outturn of revenue and expenditure for a particular financial year is endorsed. Normally the Council would recommend without comment that the discharge be granted and the debate would move to the EP as the institution with the sole authority to grant or refuse the discharge. On this occasion, in relation to 1987, the Council prefaced its recommendation with a statement on the campaign against fraud and irregularities.

The Commission, for its part, reacted both in the budgetary and legislative frameworks.   It proposed the entry of 70 million ecus in the 1990 budget to finance fraud prevention measures, a proposal which both the Council and the Parliament subsequently supported. It also presented to the Council a 45-point action programme, outlining its own suggestions for fraud prevention, improved cooperation between itself and national authorities and counteraction that the Commission itself might undertake.[5]

The action programme was particularly extensive in its coverage. It pointed to the existence of new working groups set up to examine the simplification of regulations and the harmonization of the rules on controls and administrative sanctions. It drew attention to a fresh proposal for a compulsory check on at least 5% of export consignments to be targeted on high value/high risk consignments. It indicated that the Commission itself was devoting increased resources to its own anti-fraud unit.

However, it will not be easy to turn this programme into effective action, whether through legislation in the Council or by changes in the behaviour of national authorities. An important reason for this is that the consensus on the need to fight fraud is not matched by agreement as to either its prime causes or the remedies required. Is it, for example, realistic to expect to be able to overcome the problem, given the existing system of price support? The Court of Auditors considered that central to the whole question was the differential between Community and world prices. With refunds as high as they are at present it is unlikely that any system will make it possible to avoid the risk of fraud and the concomitant budgetary burden. Moreover, the Court expressed its doubts as to whether any system which applied a differentiated rate of refund could hope to operate successfully and in a way which would be resistant to determined attempts at fraud. It noted, for example, that the nomenclature for export refunds contains 80 different classifications for beef and that the rates of refund can vary according to the country of final destination with the world divided into 11 zones, each of which has a significantly different rate.

Whose competence?
No doubt clearer legislation as proposed by the Commission would go some way to resolve this particular difficulty. However, the problem is a much wider one which has at its heart the demarcation between Community and national competences. This can be illustrated by examining the basic regulation governing agricultural markets, No. 729/70. Article 8 of this regulation specifies that the member states are responsible for ensuring that agricultural expenditure has been used for the purposes intended, for identifying and pursuing irregularities and for recovering sums lost as a result of irregularities or negligence. Their only obligation towards the Community consists in informing the Commission of the action they have taken and in particular, how far they have proceeded in taking legal proceedings against offenders. At the same time, all the financial consequences of irregularities or negligence are borne by the Community, except where they are attributable to the administrations of the member states.

This imbalance between the responsibilities of the Community and those of the member states is one which any attempt to combat fraud has to address. One can argue that it needs to be corrected by obliging the member states at least to share the financial burden of fraud or alternatively that the Commission should be given certain direct powers in relation to recovery. Neither solution is without controversy.

It is possible to envisage a system which would withhold the payment of Community advances to a value equivalent to that subject to investigation. In 1987, for example, 385 irregularities amounting to 87.4 million ecus were reported but only 1.3 million ecus were recovered in the course of the year.[6] The member states could be asked to forgo the amount remaining (86.1 million ecus) until the recovery procedures had been completed. However, there must be some considerable doubt as to the usefulness of this approach. It would not only create a disincentive to further reporting of irregularities but would fail to address the problem as a whole, given that it is universally acknowledged that fraud extends far beyond the cases reported.

It may therefore be more fruitful to look at the way the existing system of recovery works. As the Commission points out, it is notoriously slow and the barriers to recovery very great:

where the sums involved are very large, the operators explore all available means to endeavour to defend themselves and the recovery procedure is generally deferred until judgement, and sometimes until appeals have been completed. The Commission has no direct power to speed up the work of the courts, which can last several years.[7]

At present, the Commission's role is very restricted once agricultural payments have been made. It is limited to recovering amounts from the member states in the context of the clearance of accounts. The amounts involved are certainly not inconsiderable: for 1986, for example, they totalled 213 million ecus or just under 1% out of a total volume of Guarantee expenditure of 21.6 billion ecus. However, the procedure relates strictly to erroneous claims where the Commission considers that the legislation has not been respected: it does not concern fraud. Moreover, although it gives rise to a number of cases of litigation in the Court of Justice, they involve the administrations of the member states and do not bring the

Commission into direct contact with those claiming Community funds.

Given the extent of the fraud problem, there are surely grounds for reviewing the role of the Commission. If it were empowered to act by a revision of Article 8 of Regulation 729/70, then the framework for it to do so would be available in the provisions of the EEC Treaty. The Treaty provides both for the right of appeal against Commission decisions and for the legal enforcement of such decisions against private parties. In accordance with Article 173 the party concerned would have two months to appeal to the Court of Justice against a Commission decision. If it failed to do so, the decision would stand. Article 192 states that 'decisions of the Council or of the Commission which impose a pecuniary obligation on persons other than States, shall be enforceable' in accordance with the rules of civil procedure in force in the state concerned. In other words, if empowered to act, the Commission would be prevented from acting arbitrarily as well as being sure that its decisions would not be ignored.

Without question, there are difficulties in this approach of empowering the Commission to act. It would involve a significant change in the balance that exists at present between the Community and the member states. In the evidence given to the British House of Lords both the Treasury Solicitor and the Serious Fraud Office were very reluctant even to entertain the idea of separate Community recovery procedures. The former argued that 'prosecutions ... should be entrusted to those familiar with and experienced in national criminal law and procedure ... in a manner consistent with public policy considerations', while the latter felt it would not be 'proper to assign an investigation into a fraud which takes place in this country to an overseas body'.[8]

However, these objections are not entirely relevant. It would not be necessary to give the Commission the power to launch national criminal investigation. It already has the right to impose administrative fines in the area of competition policy, and the change envisaged here would simply be extending that legal mechanism into another field which is already governed by EEC law. Moreover, the change would be without prejudice to the member states' right or indeed duty to initiate any criminal prosecutions on the national level.

The member states themselves are coming to recognize that it is not enough to insist on national prerogatives and that the existing arrangements are often unsatisfactory. An illustration of this arose during the negotiations on the revision of the regulation governing the collection of traditional own resources. The Commission had pressed for the right to be able to undertake on-the-spot checks in the member states but the Council was initially opposed to such an idea. However, in the conciliation meeting with the Parliament it changed its mind and included such a provision in the regulation adopted.[9]

This willingness to act at Community level can partly be explained by a recognition of the inadequacy of a purely national approach. Even if individual member states take a tougher approach to the policing of CAP frauds, with more checks on the quantity and quality of stocks, this cannot of itself guarantee a common system which does not discriminate against one country over another. To put it more bluntly, the burden will fall on those who seek to combat fraud, rather than those who take a more relaxed attitude to it. Hence there has to be some wider framework which would necessarily extend Community competences. Take, for example, the proposal referred to earlier which would require member states to carry out a minimum level of physical inspections of exports attracting Community refunds. Who other than a Community institution could verify whether the obligation was being met? Moreover, it would make little sense to carry out such inspections if more success in uncovering fraud were not matched by pressure to pursue guilty parties with greater determination than at present. In other words, successful implementation of this more limited measure would lead naturally to a change in the recovery procedures towards involving the Community more directly.

Structural spending
In the course of the negotiations leading up to the decision to double

the size of the structural funds, those advocating the increase devoted remarkably little time to asking what the extra resources would be used for. It became an article of faith whereby it was assumed that such an increase must be beneficial, particularly for the poorer member states faced with the prospect of opening their markets in the run-up to 1992.

There is no doubt that considerable potential has been created by the increase. It will release about 55,000 million ecus or more than £35 billion over the period from 1988 to 1992. However, it is worth recalling that there have been significant increases in the funds in the past. The regional fund, for example, grew from 836 million ecus (in payments) in 1979 to 2,980 million ecus in 1988, thereby releasing 15.6 billion ecus over the ten-year period. This did not insulate the fund from criticism. In his testimony to the British House of Lords, John Hume, the SDLP MEP from Northern Ireland, went so far as to argue that 'there never was a regional policy at all, it was a Regional Fund operated on a Red Cross basis, with handouts here and there'.[10] The Select Committee concurred, suggesting in their conclusions that:

> . . . in the past the Council of Ministers have not given the Structural Funds the consideration they deserved. Little thought has been given to the purpose of the Funds. They have been treated as little more than a means of transferring resources from one member state to another, with no consistent concern for results. The share-out was essentially political.[11]

An opportunity to rectify this situation had already presented itself with the entry into force of the Single European Act. Article 130 D specified the need 'to clarify and rationalize' the tasks of the Funds , 'to increase their efficiency and to coordinate their activities between themselves and with the operation of the existing financial instruments'. Following the Brussels European Council this injunction was acted upon when the three structural funds were linked together around five objectives.[12] Moreover, Regulation No. 2052/88 adopted in June 1988 and Regulation No. 4253/88 of December 1988 laid down a very different structure of operation from that which had prevailed in the past.

The most significant element in these measures was that they moved the emphasis of Community activity from detailed projects to wider programmes. Under the old system, the Commission was faced with thousands of projects which it had to process individually. In 1988, for example, 3,841 investment projects received grants totalling 3.8 billion ecus. This should be a thing of the past. Under the new system the member states submit to the Commission plans for the regions that are eligible for assistance and these plans are in turn incorporated into *Community support frameworks* lasting for three to five years. The Commission will therefore be working on a much smaller number of dossiers.

A new role for the Commission?
This change in emphasis will bring with it a change in the character of the work of the Commission. Whereas before it was confronted with a mass of demands which it could do little more than register, it now has the opportunity to examine the plans presented by the member states and to express an opinion as to which parts of them it wishes to support in drawing up the Community support frameworks. In the past there was no basis on which to assess a project as it came forward in isolation; now it will be possible to obtain an overall view and to make an informed choice. In other words, the Commission will be much more concerned with negotiation of terms, a more complex task than that undertaken in the past.

It ought, for example, to be easier to apply the additionality principle than it was in the past. Article 9 of Regulation No. 4253/88 specifies that the Commission and the member states must ensure that the increase in the funds should have 'a genuine additional economic impact in the regions concerned and result in at least an equivalent increase in the total volume of official or similar (Community and national) structural aid in the Member State concerned, taking into account the macro-economic circumstances in which the funding takes place'. On this basis the Commission is enabled to compare the amount provided in the course of the implementation of a particular Community support framework with the amount of aid provided to the region concerned before. As a result, the point of comparison will be previous levels of expenditure rather than the contribution made by a member state to a project which also receives Community support. In principle, at least, the Commission will have a much better overview of what is going on than it did in the past. This in turn should allow it to devote more attention to ensuring that the extra finance does not simply go towards nationally defined objectives but also permits the application of Community criteria, which might otherwise be overlooked. Thus, there can be additionality of objectives as well as of finance.

There can, however, be no certainty that the new system will work as smoothly as suggested. Any system that operates on the basis of set criteria is certain to provoke disagreement over the way in which the criteria are applied. Past experience with the funds has demonstrated this point very clearly. Take, for example, the regulation in favour of Greece on exceptional financial support in the social field. This regulation was approved in 1984 and was designed to permit Greece to improve its system of vocational training in urban centres as well as that for the rehabilitation of the mentally handicapped. An indicative amount of 120 million ecus was included in the regulation for the period January 1984 to December 1988 but in the first four years of its application, payments did not exceed 21.7 million ecus (i.e. 18% of the total), while only 25 of the 224 projects agreed by the Commission were completed.

As a result, on a request from the Greek government, the Commission proposed and the Council agreed (Reg. No. 4130/88 of 16 December 1988) that the duration of the regulation be extended to the end of 1991 so as to give more time for the appropriations envisaged to be spent. At the same time, the criteria for obtaining assistance were relaxed so that Community monies could be used to cover the acquisition of sites for construction or of existing buildings for the purposes of extension and/or renovation. This relaxation of the criteria was justified by the considerable administrative and financial difficulties faced by the Greek authorities but it constituted a marked departure from the rules applicable elsewhere, notably in the regional fund, which does not permit the use of Community funds for land acquisition.[13]

This example raises a general issue which is not restricted to one country or one set of regulations. Certainly there is no reason to suppose that the problem has disappeared as a result of the reform of the funds. Member states are sure to remain reticent about allowing the Commission extensive discretion. They continue to think in terms of the need to maximize the benefits accruing to them and to guarantee that the existing balance of advantage not be disturbed. Immediately in January 1989 the indicative division of the appropriations in the regional fund for Objective No. 1 (Promoting the development of less-developed regions) prompted a negative reaction from Italy because it felt that the calculations used by the Commission (based on national GNP rather than the per capita GNP of the regions concerned) penalized the Mezzogiorno, the poor regions of southern Italy.

Moreover, the experience so far with integrated development programmes and integrated operations – the prototypes of the programme approach – has not been a dramatic success. The Court of Auditors has been particularly critical. It considered that funds were spent without objectives being defined, reports to monitor progress were not made and a lack of co-ordination prevented true 'integration' between projects.[14]

Given the powerful political pressures and the organizational difficulties, it is certainly dangerous to assume that the funds can be managed on a more efficient basis. However, as the amounts involved increase, so the incentive for all states, not just those benefiting most directly, to devise adequate mechanisms of financial management will surely increase. If this is the case, then what is the alternative to giving broader discretion to the Commission? If it is not to be allowed to assess the plans put to it, then it would be better not to maintain the pretence of Community criteria and to transfer the extra finance available directly. Such was the tenor of the proposal made, for example, by the Centre for European Policy Studies, which suggested that direct financial transfers could play a role on the 'bottom line' of the regional fund.

If, for any reason, a Member State failed to take up its project allocation within a given year, it could eventually, under well-defined conditions, receive at least a proportion of the balance in the form of a direct financial transfer. Then, if there were major differences between Member States, in their ability to absorb or to administer regional fund expenditures, the inter-country pattern of policy intervention would nevertheless approximate to the desired inter-country pattern to promote convergence.[15]

It is, however, surely too late to follow this path. The commitment to making the funds more efficient and more effective has been too firmly established for it to be easy to envisage that finance could be made available independently of proposals for action. For example, it is now specified that the ERDF contribution to Objective 1 areas can vary between 50 and 75% and between 25 and 50% in other areas. This is in marked contrast with the old regulation which specified that the amount coming from the Community could vary only between 50 and 55%. The reason for the wider span can be traced back to the differences between the member states in the Council but the consequence is necessarily to accentuate the pressures for negotiated arrangements between Commission and member states.

The Commission itself may find this new arrangement less than comfortable, at least in the early stages. It was familiar with the old system and may have found it reasonably congenial not to have to use an undue level of discretion. However, it must surely be in the interests of the Community to ensure that the Commission does develop the means to negotiate effectively with the member states and that both parties do their utmost to ensure that the plans adopted do have a recognizable economic impact.

What this chapter has suggested is that the decisions taken at the Brussels European Council have helped to direct attention to the quality of Community spending and away from the issue of quantity. This was doubtless not an entirely conscious choice but was a product of the consensus reached on the expansion of the budget. However, this does not mean that the Community will only be concerned with the efficient management of funds over the period up to 1992. The shape of the budget will return to the agenda long before the present financial perspective expires.

5
DEVELOPING NEW POLICIES

In the enthusiasm that surrounded the agreement reached at the Brussels European Council, there was a certain element of self-delusion as to the permanence of the financial structure established. As the months have passed since February 1988 it has become clearer that the debate on the Community budget is far from over. With the approach of 1992 one can expect a renewed struggle over future financing which will certainly require a fresh consensus to be reached within the European Council.

The nature of the difficulties ahead can be illuminated by considering three specific gaps in the financial perspective that forms part of the interinstitutional agreement. First, it has become clear that the amounts entered in certain categories are not sufficient to cover all the existing commitments of the Community. Second, the evolution of the Community's GNP has created space within the annual ceilings, which make it possible to foresee higher levels of spending than originally envisaged. Third and perhaps most importantly, the perspective does not extend beyond 1992, nor does the agreement provide a mechanism whereby medium-term financial planning can be carried forward on a rolling basis.

It would be illusory to suppose that there is no urgency about confronting these difficulties: they will come on to the political agenda long before 1992. The first two have already prompted calls for revision of the financial perspective. Indeed, the unexpected developments in Eastern Europe led the budgetary authority to decide on a revision specifically linked to increased aid for Poland and Hungary before the end of the 1990 budgetary procedure. In this way, only 18 months after the signature of the agreement, paragraph 12 was invoked and used. A revision of the perspective took place 'by a joint decision of the two arms of the budgetary authority, acting on a proposal from the Commission'.

The third and last difficulty, the shape of the post-1992 settlement, will also not wait for a solution. As the single market becomes more of a reality, so it will become increasingly important to determine the policy structure within which that market will be expected to operate. This need not necessarily mean a major increase in resources as measured against GNP, but it will require decisions as to the balance to be achieved between different areas of expenditure.

The shortfall in the perspective

Already in the course of 1989 budgetary procedure it became clear that it would not be possible to achieve all the Community's objectives within the structure provided for by the financial perspective. Two particular cases will be discussed here, both of which show the limits of trying to apply that perspective in too rigid a fashion.

The food aid issue

The first case concerns the appropriations needed to purchase Community food aid on world markets. It has already been noted that the rise in the value of the dollar in relation to the ecu had a dramatic downward effect on the cost of the agricultural policy. At the same time, however, it became increasingly expensive for the Community to meet the commitments it had made to third countries for the supply of food aid. In principle, a solution to this problem existed in that the greater cost of food aid was closely matched by a decrease in the level of appropriations needed to cover export restitutions in relation to food aid. A transfer within the budget appeared therefore to offer a way out without increasing the overall level of appropriations.

However, such a solution was considerably hindered by the

provision in the interinstitutional agreement that the sub-ceilings for the various categories in the financial perspective cannot be exceeded. Thus whereas the appropriations for food aid are to be found in Chapter 92 in the budget which comes under category 4 'Other Policies', export restitutions in relation to food aid are financed from Article 292, which is covered by category 1 'EAGGF Guarantee'. A transfer would therefore not only mean a reduction in the level of compulsory expenditure in favour of non-compulsory (something the Council has always been very reluctant to authorize) but would also threaten to take spending under category 4 beyond the ceiling laid down in the perspective.

The Council recognized that there was a problem in meeting the tonnage targets set but was not immediately prepared to commit itself to finding the appropriations necessary. However, at the beginning of 1989 negotiations began between the Council and the Parliament to try to resolve the issue. In April they succeeded in coming to an arrangement whereby both parties agreed to the principle of proposals for transfer from Article 292 to Chapter 92, noting that the combined appropriations of the two articles would be sufficient to meet the food aid programme agreed for the year.[1]

However, the agreement was not watertight. When the Commission did come forward with a proposal for transfer, the amount involved did take the expenditure under category 4 beyond the figure contained in the perspective and provoked strong reserves in the Council. There was, however, no qualified majority against the proposal and so with the EP in favour, it was adopted. In this way, the perspective was obliged to bend to broader considerations of Community policy.

Of course, it is possible to argue that this case will not constitute a precedent and such indeed was the line of the Council in the agreement it reached with the Parliament. But in the Community it is always unwise to state that something is not to be considered as a precedent. It almost certainly will be! This example is no exception. It leaves unresolved what will happen in subsequent years if once again the rise in the value of the dollar makes it impossible to maintain commitments to third countries. Will the Council be prepared to risk the opprobrium of refusing to grant extra appropriations to maintain a fixed volume of food aid or alternatively of reducing the volume of aid so as to respect the financial perspective? Neither option seems very attractive after the concession made in the spring of 1989.

Administrative expenditure

The food aid issue has the merit of not involving an increase in the overall volume of appropriations. The Community's objectives can be met by redistribution within the categories of the financial perspective. This is not the case with the appropriations available for administrative expenditure. This expenditure was grouped in the perspective inside category 5 with two very different kinds of expenditure, namely that for repayments to member states and for destocking. Although the amount available for financing the disposal of existing stocks up to 1992 was fixed, the repayments to member states can only be estimated and depend in any case on the size of the budgets voted. Hence not only is the precise amount available for administration not visible, it cannot be precisely determined in advance. Nevertheless, there is no question that the amount available is not sufficient to cover the projected needs of the institutions up to 1992. In 1992, for the financial perspective to be respected, administrative expenditure would have to drop substantially, to below the figure it reached in 1988. This could be particularly embarrassing for the Council, which is committed to the buying of a new building in Brussels for which it requires rates of increase in its budget over the period up to 1992 which go well beyond anything that the other institutions are seeking.

This might not seem in itself a very major issue in the context of the overall development of the Community were it not for possibilities for linkage between issues. Once the need for revision of the perspective is acknowledged in one area, a general debate about the volume of appropriations to be allocated to all the other categories is unavoidable.

The evolution of GNP

The decision to link the Community's finances to the GNP of the Twelve is proving increasingly controversial. When it was established, it was seen as helping to guarantee budgetary security up to 1992, but its importance extended much further. In particular, it generated a certain level of expectations as to the amount of resources that the Community could expect to have available in the future. The European Parliament, for example, was strongly opposed to the imposition of annual ceilings but could at least welcome a system that made the overall level of revenue independent of any one of the individual components of revenue.

What has now emerged is that, owing to more rapid growth than expected in the Community economy, the Commission expects to be able to meet existing objectives at levels of GNP significantly below those originally envisaged. This is very clear from the table in Annex IV, which indicates the shape of the financial perspective after adaptation by the Commission in the spring of 1989. The table shows first, that the budgets for 1988 and 1989 were both agreed at levels below the ceiling of own resources laid down and second, that the budgets for the coming years will require a substantially lower level of appropriations than that available under the own resources decision. Thus the 1988 payment appropriations corresponded to 1.11% rather than 1.12% of GNP, while in 1989 the difference between the two figures rose to 0.04% of GNP as the payments needed fell to 1.10% of GNP. The Commission and the budgetary authority expected the trend to continue: payments for 1990, 1991 and 1992 were anticipated to fall 0.03%, 0.03% and 0.04% respectively, below the GNP percentage figure contained in the perspective as agreed in the summer of 1988. In fact, the gap for 1990 grew wider as a result of the agricultural savings and the improvement in Community GNP. The Council set the 1990 draft budget at first reading at 0.98% of GNP, but by the end of the procedure the own resources required had actually fallen to 0.95%. The difference between the figure for 1990 as envisaged in 1988 and the actual figure voted in the budget had thus expanded to 0.2% of GNP or the equivalent of around 10 billion ecus.

The importance of these developments arises from the fact that the financial perspective in its original form exhausted all the resources available within the resource ceiling with the exception of the 0.03% margin for unforeseen expenditure. Now, there is a very significant percentage of GNP available beyond the 0.03% margin. Although the Council and the Parliament were both prepared to accept the adjusted figures for 1990 in the spring of 1989, this consensus did not survive the arrival of the third directly elected Parliament.

In the autumn of 1989, the EP drew attention to the very significant level of resources available below the GNP ceiling and linked it to pressure for a revision of the perspective to cover the unexpected situation in Eastern Europe as well as those new policies which it wished to encourage. On both fronts, it proved remarkably successful.

In relation to aid to Poland and Hungary, it first called on the Commission to quantify the level of aid required to fulfil the mandate given to it at the Paris Summit in June 1989 to coordinate efforts to Eastern Europe. It then insisted that not only should the amount proposed by the Commission, and accepted by the Council, be increased from 200 to 300 million ecus but also that it should be covered by an upward revision of category 4 of the financial perspective before the end of 1989. The Council, for its part, recognised the political importance of the issue and conceded not only the increase but also the revision of the perspective required to finance it.

As for the revision of the perspective to cover new policies, the Parliament succeeded in obtaining a firm commitment from the Commission that it would present a major proposal for such a revision in February 1990 for both 1991 and 1992. In the process, it gave a clear picture of the areas in which it expected such a revision to be concentrated, drawing particular attention to the development of transport, energy and environment policies. The Council, for its part, was more reluctant to indicate its attitude towards such a revision but it did suggest that it was prepared to consider increased aid for Eastern Europe for subsequent years as well as for 1990, to take account of the dramatic pace of change.

The agenda for the 1990 revision will also take into account the extent to which the commitments entered into in 1988 have been implemented. It will be recalled, for example, that in 1989 the Commission decided only to carry over 48 million ecus in differentiated payment appropriations but at the same time it cancelled 509 million ecus, which would have been carried over automatically under the old system. This amount was not added to the 1990 financial perspective, as one might have expected in the light of the provision for transfers under paragraph 11 of the interinstitutional agreement. However, one must assume that the commitments to which they are linked must be honoured before 1992 and if so, the corresponding payments will have to be added to the perspective of 1991 or 1992 if the effective doubling of the funds is to be honoured.

The major issue, though, is likely to be that the present perspective allows very little room for the expansion of non-compulsory expenditure at a time when there is a very considerable leeway below the GNP ceilings. Within category 4, the increases at present envisaged are 57 million ecus between 1990 and 1991 and 60 million ecus between 1991 and 1992 (in commitments at 1989 prices). The decisions of the Council have themselves already put pressure on this small degree of expansion. In March 1988, for example, the Industry Council agreed on a package of social measures in the steel sector, at a cost of 150 million ecus over the four-year period up to 1991. Although the bulk of the financing is to come from the ECSC budget (110 million ecus), the possibility that a part of the appropriations would come from the general budget has not been excluded. The same argument applies with still greater force to the Lingua programme, a programme designed to encourage the teaching of foreign languages in the Community, that was approved by the education ministers in May 1989. In Britain this proposal was controversial because of the content of the scheme and its implication that the Community become involved in the national school systems. However, what received rather less attention was the fact that a programme costing 200 million ecus for the five years from 1990 had been agreed apparently without any undue concern as to whether the finance was available within category 4 of the financial perspective.

This apparent insouciance of the Council is particularly odd given the provisions of the decision on budgetary discipline (see Annex II, Article 16), whereby no Council decision which requires finance beyond that available in the budget or the financial perspective can be implemented without amendment of the budget or the perspective. This provision was in fact designed to give further protection to the non-compulsory sector vis-à-vis agriculture. However, it is a general injunction which would, for example, make the implementation of the Lingua programme impossible without revision of the perspective, if it cannot be financed within the existing category 4 ceiling.

We must next consider the prospects for such a revision. Article 12 of the interinstitutional agreement, as already indicated, specifies that any revision can only be made by a joint decision of the two arms of the budgetary authority, acting on a proposal from the Commission. It therefore depends not only on the willingness of the Commission to bring a proposal forward but also on the readiness of the Council to enter into serious negotiations with the Parliament. The fact that the Council agreed to a revision in December 1989 and was not able to exclude the possibility of a further review of expenditure linked to external developments, particularly in Eastern Europe, is likely to give the Council a stake in some form of revision in the spring of 1990. The issue then is: what sort of revision? At one level, the agreement does provide a basis for negotiations. As Article 8 indicates, the Parliament, the Council and the Commission are committed to a 'better balance' between the various categories of expenditure. However, this provision was designed primarily to ensure that any increase in compulsory expenditure could not take place at the expense of the non-compulsory sector. In the meantime, as we have seen, the possibility of an overrun in agricultural expenditure has receded sharply. In the 1990 budget, EAGGF Guarantee at 26.5 billion ecus accounts for only 54% of the total volume of commitments: this represents a stabilization in money terms in relation to 1989 and thus a reduction in real terms. In this way, a 'better balance' has already come about without any need for a revision and weakened the case for invoking paragraph 8.

Under these circumstances, the Parliament will seek to use the argument of increased headroom within the GNP ceiling to justify the largest possible revision, while the Council will want to limit it as far as possible. An agreement could be envisaged in terms of a trade-off between the interests of the two parties. If, for example, the revision is designed primarily to strengthen 'privileged' non-compulsory expenditure, then the Parliament may not find itself without allies in the Council. Much as the EP objected to the creation of this category, it expanded the area of the budget in which a number of member states considered that they had a very important interest. Hence if significant delays do emerge in the use of the appropriations set aside for economic and social cohesion, the countries concerned are certain to want to take every possible step to ensure that the doubling of the funds is not put at risk. In that process the EP may also be able to secure at least some of its demands in relation to category 4 expenditure.

After 1992
One very significant feature of the financial perspective is that it does not extend beyond 1992. Although the interinstitutional agreement provides for annual updating (paragraph 9), this only applies to the existing text. As the Parliament's report proposing ratification of the agreement noted:

the annual updating of the financial perspective does not include the entering of amounts for the fifth year, which would have made it possible to plan expenditure beyond 1992 on a 'sliding' basis: 1988–1992, 1989–1993, etc.[2]

The reason for this failure is clear: the consensus that was reached at the Brussels European Council did not extend beyond 1992. There was no agreement, and no attempt to seek an agreement, on what the Community would or should look like several years in advance. Although there was unanimity on the need to create a single market, this concealed strong differences as to the conditions necessary for such a market to come into being as well as the developments to which its creation might lead.

However, this does not mean that the shape of the perspective will be considered sacrosanct until 1992, or indeed up to the end of 1991, by which time the Commission has been invited to submit a report on the operation of the own resource system.[3] It has already been noted that the agreement to double the structural funds referred to the period from 1988 to 1993 so that a large component of an updated perspective has already been agreed. Other components of the perspective will become clearer as an inevitable consequence of the legislative timetable. As the first footnote to the perspective indicates, both the R&D programme and the IMPs are due to be renegotiated for the period after 1991. As it would have looked extremely odd to leave a blank for category 3 in 1992, it was agreed to enter a figure which is more than double that which was estimated to be necessary at the time of the agreement but with the proviso that 'only expenditure for which a legal basis exists may be financed under this heading'. In principle, therefore, the remainder would lapse if no legal base were agreed beforehand. The reality is that negotiations on a new framework programme began in the second half of 1989 and are likely to lead to an agreement on a new volume of resources for the period from 1992 onwards. Under these circumstances, substantial progress would have been made in updating the perspective at least for 1993, especially if the GNP figures continue to be so favourable and to suggest that extra finance could be found within the 1.2% ceiling on own resources.

However, this can only provide a pragmatic first step. It ignores the substantial pressure that exists for the development of new policy initiatives. In its report on future financing of the Community (COM(87)101), the Commission proposed that significant appropriations for new policies be entered in the budget for the period between 1988 and 1992, the amount rising from 500 million ecus to 2,800 million ecus (in commitments). The European Parliament, for its part, strongly supported this position though considering the amounts proposed rather low. In the discussions which took place on the interinstitutional agreement, the Council firmly resisted any attempts to include a separate category for new policies in the financial perspective, basing itself entirely on the conclusions of the European Council. However, the Commission and the Parliament were successful in obtaining one reference to such policies in the interinstitutional agreement. Thus, the first part of paragraph 6 states:

The financial perspective 1988 to 1992 indicates, in commitment appropriations, the volume and breakdown of foreseeable Community expenditure, *including that for the development of new policies* [author's italics].

Such a provision might not appear to have any very important effect, given that it implies that new policies have to be covered by category 4 of the financial perspective, where non-compulsory expenditure is anticipated to increase by relatively small amounts and therefore the room for any new policies is strictly limited. To accept this would, however, be to adopt an extremely static analysis of the financial perspective and the way in which it is likely to develop.

The 1990 budgetary procedure showed the determination of the European Parliament to advance the debate on new policies, and the issue of aid to Poland and Hungary provided a mechanism for bringing that debate to the front of the political agenda. New demands served as a means of putting pressure on an existing framework. The situation was particularly awkward for countries like Britain, politically committed to assisting Eastern Europe but also very reluctant to expand Community spending. However, it was not a new situation as Britain has proved consistently slow in recognizing the strength of pressure for new expenditure at Community level. After the SEA came into force in 1987, there was considerable reluctance to acknowledge that the concept of economic and social cohesion was more than a rhetorical device. Lynda Chalker, for example, then Minister of State in the Foreign and Commonwealth Office responsible for the EC, stated in evidence to the House of Lords Select Committee of the European Communities in advance of the Brussels European Council that a further growth in the structural funds was not ruled out, but that they would have to 'grow in line with the maximum rate, which is the the growth which the Community can reasonably afford each year'.[4] After the event it is easy to claim that this was a negotiating position and that Britain was forced to give it up in the European Council bargaining. However, the effect of this position was to make it more difficult to influence the shape of the increased expenditure that was agreed. Will this mistake be repeated in the post-1992 debate?

There is no question that the present British government has taken a narrowly focused and primarily deregulatory view of what a single market should involve. Above all, it is not seen as having a necessary link with other policies which have expenditure implications. In contrast Jacques Delors has eloquently argued the case for linking the completion of the single market with the development of other common policies:

> We cannot want the benefits of the great internal market
> without thinking at the same time and to the same degree about
> the deepening of the common policies which make it possible:
> strengthening of economic and monetary cooperation; taking
> into account the social dimension; elaboration of an external
> identity for the Community in commercial and financial affairs.[5]

In the face of these conflicting conceptions of the future it would be perverse, if not futile, to take a stand based on the total respect of the maximum rate provisions governing the growth of the non-compulsory sector. Rather the debate has to be broadened to identify what the Council will consider privileged NCE in the years after 1992. This debate has been effectively launched by the report on economic and monetary union, chaired by Jacques Delors. It argues very strongly that such a union could not avoid taking responsibility for ensuring balanced development throughout the Community. This must involve financial assistance to those regions at the periphery which are likely to suffer as transport costs and economies of scale tend to favour a shift in economic activity towards the highly developed areas at the centre. Hence the commitment to at least maintaining the present effort in relation to economic and social cohesion. However, the report also makes clear (in paragraph 29) that there should not be excessive reliance on such assistance. To improve market efficiency it would be important to develop other instruments, among which it identifies infrastructure, research and technological development, and the environment.

The debate about economic and monetary union will therefore have important repercussions on the budget. It is already creating an environment in which those outside government are seeing the possibility of operating at a European level and seeking Community support in the process. A good example is transport where there has been an increasing awareness that weaknesses in infrastructure may make it more difficult to achieve a single market. In January 1989 the national railway companies of the Twelve, plus those of Switzerland and Austria, submitted to the Commission a report on a large-scale project for a European high-speed train network. They estimated the global cost of this project at around 90 billion ecus and argued that there should be some financial support at Community level. Subsequently in March the European Round Table of industrialists made a more general plea for the renewal of transport infrastructure. They noted that while traffic had increased by 25% between 1975 and 1985, the level of investment in infrastructure had fallen from 1.5% to 0.9% of the GNP of the states concerned. They even went so far as to propose the creation of a European Infrastructure Agency with the task of coordinating major projects in this area.[6] The importance of such ideas is not simply that they are coming from outside the Community institutions but that they are being couched in the language of the commitments of the SEA. This assures them a degree of support that they would not otherwise have enjoyed.

There are also issues which all are eager to be seen to be responding to. The obvious example is the environment, which has combined a powerful political lobby with a widespread recognition that the problems involved cannot be resolved at national level. The greatest financial impact arising out of this new situation will be felt not by the Community budget but by producers and consumers. Thus the compromise reached in the Council in June 1989 on exhaust emissions for small cars will increase substantially the costs for manufacturers as well as making cars more expensive.

However, this does not mean that there will not be demands for increased expenditure at Community level. Two sorts of expenditure can be envisaged. First, the establishment of common rules generates pressure for ensuring that the rules are respected. Hence the European Commission proposed and the Council, in November 1989, agreed the establishment of a European Environmental Agency whose task it will be to collect information, designed to help the Commission to supervise the uniform application of agreed

61

standards. Its establishment will imply an adequate administrative budget to enable it to fulfil its functions. Second, one can anticipate proposals intended to encourage the respect of community rules by making a contribution to those states for whom such respect poses difficulties. Such kinds of expenditure are already part of the community debate. In December 1988, for example, the Commission made a proposal for a financial contribution from the Community towards expenditure incurred by member states in seeking to ensure respect of the Community rules for the conservation and management of fishery resources.[7] Moreover one year later, in November 1989, the Council not only endorsed the principle of such expenditure but agreed a package worth 110 million ecus over five years from January 1991. The move to Community rules on the environment seems very likely to involve similar claims on the budget.

These examples do not guarantee that the financial perspective established in the summer of 1988 will be updated for the years after 1992. The agreement that was reached then was based on a delicate compromise. It gave satisfaction to those concerned to ensure the opening of markets as well to those determined to ensure that such policies of market-opening did not adversely affect them. It satisfied the advocates of budgetary discipline as well as those eager to benefit from Community support. Such a compromise will be difficult to reconstruct but it would be wrong to underestimate the power of custom and practice in the life of the Community. All Community institutions have benefited from the relative calm generated by the 1988 agreement. Which institution will want to put that *acquis* at risk without having exhausted all possible means of finding an entente?

6
CONCLUSIONS

The discussion so far has suggested four main conclusions: first, that the Brussels European Council of February 1988 did bring about very significant changes in the volume and composition of Community revenue, in the pattern of expenditure to which that revenue be put and in the relations between the Council and the Parliament; second, that the achievement of the commitments entered into at that meeting is not yet guaranteed, whether one is referring to the control of agricultural expenditure or to the doubling of the funds; third, that the resource security attained has directed attention more clearly to the way in which those resources are used and to the role that the Community institutions should play in ensuring that they are managed wisely; and finally, that the consensus reached at Brussels, embodied in the financial perspective, will have to be renegotiated in advance of 1992 as the debate about the financing necessary to enable a single market to operate intensifies and the pressure for new policy initiatives increases.

However, all of this discussion has taken a relatively narrow budgetary focus and it may be useful to conclude with a number of broader observations about the role of the budget and its relationship to the Community as a whole. This chapter will consider these issues by examining the way in which particular interests in the EC interrelate with the collective interest. It will take as its starting-point the claim that such a collective interest does exist and is more than the sum of the particular interests that compose the Community. It will suggest that such a claim is of more than academic concern and has a direct relation to the policy-making process. It will argue that it is becoming increasingly important to take decisions which take account of the way in which the Community agenda is broadening and acquiring a shape that escapes the control of any one member state.

This line of argument has a particular relevance in the British context. It is peculiarly hard to persuade a British audience of the existence of a collective Community interest. Either it is dismissed as a vague notion, concealing the struggle of individual interests, or it is defined as the product of the decision-making process, such that what the Community decides corresponds to what is in its interest. Rarely is it perceived as a standard against which the future development of the Community can be judged. The source of this way of thinking need not be debated here: opposition to power-sharing below or above the national level or the weakness of the idea of the state, embodying a willingness to pursue collective values, offer two interpretations which can be suggested.[1] However, the consequences of the approach cannot be under-estimated. It has prompted an unwillingness to look very far into the future combined with an exaggerated determination to take discrete steps founded in pragmatism. If the analysis of this chapter is correct, then such behaviour in future is likely to be the source of unnecessary friction within the Community at a time of important new developments.

The purpose of the budget
This debate can be set in a more concrete framework if we begin by considering what the Community budget is designed to do.[2] First, it is more than a device enabling member states to achieve their objectives more effectively. The very existence of a budget with a degree of autonomy has an important integrative function, binding member states together. The fact that commonly agreed policies are paid for out of a common budget - rather than by coordinating national expenditure - makes it more difficult for member states to bend the rules and can provide a basis for Community monitoring and investigation, as suggested in Chapter 3. Moreover, common

funds encourage a perception that expenditure which may not be justifiable in national terms may well be so if considered in a wider Community framework.

Second, it is insufficient to argue that the budget is simply an allocative device, intended to distribute resources in as efficient a way as possible. It also has a wider purpose, as a mechanism of redistribution, designed to divert resources consciously from richer to poorer states. This has always been the case throughout the history of the Community. Structural spending, whether in the agricultural, social or regional sector, was specifically designed to help the poorer regions of the Community. Even EAGGF Guarantee spending was intended to protect a declining sector of the economy, though its impact was to prove much wider and less controllable.

However, the constant difficulty was that the resources available were too small to effect a major element of redistribution. In part, for this reason, there has been a tendency, particularly in Britain, to underestimate the importance of the redistributive function and to suggest that there is no reason for it to seek to acquire a more developed redistributive function. This restricted view of the budget's role is accompanied by a stress on the idea that the real character of the budget can be identified by looking at the 'profit' and 'loss' of each country. On this basis the Community debate on the budget can be fully explained in terms of the financial return that each country makes from it.

No one would wish to deny that the Community has to take account of the balance of advantage that it offers to the member states and that this balance has to include payments from the budget. The range of 'public goods' that it at present provides is too limited for budgetary imbalances to be ignored. Very major differences do remain between what each member state receives through the Community budget and what each contributes in the form of own resources, as Table 5 indicates. Thus, despite the arrangements made for the British rebate, the United Kingdom still receives a markedly smaller fraction of allocated expenditure than it contributes in own resources. Only Germany is in a less favourable position with a percentage gap almost double that of Britain.

65

Table 5   Payments to Member States and own resources from Member States (1987)

	Payments		Own Resources	
	million ecus	%	million ecus	%
Belgium	985.4	3.2	1,702.6	4.8
Denmark	1,144.2	3.7	844.7	2.4
France	6,744.3	21.9	7,330.0	20.7
Greece	1,876.9	6.1	340.4	1.0
Ireland	1,438.0	4.7	337.5	1.0
Italy	5,256.2	17.1	5,191.6	14.7
Luxembourg	12.0	–	73.5	0.2
Netherlands	2,890.2	9.4	2,366.2	6.7
Portugal	731.4	2.4	341.8	1.0
Spain	1,984.8	6.4	1,708.7	4.8
United Kingdom	3,121.5	10.1	5,727.5	16.2
West Germany	4,541.8	14.7	9,384.6	26.5
Total	30,812 (inc. 85.3 where allocation not available)		35,349	

Source: Court of Auditors (1988): *Annual Report Concerning the Financial Year 1987*, pp. 224–5.

Such a table is important in influencing the budgetary argument. This was obvious when the Commission presented its proposals on the shape of the revenue system (see above, pp. 14–16). They were designed to take account of relative prosperity but at the same time threatened to change the balance of advantage. The Commission calculated that Italy, for example, would have had to contribute 188 million ecus extra to finance the 1987 budget, whereas Britain would have contributed 106 million ecus less.[3] Not surprisingly, the Italians were in the forefront of those determined to modify the Commission proposals and they were successful in so doing.

However, to point to such examples of countries defending their corner is not to prove that the Community budget can be considered simply in terms of profit and loss. The reason why solutions were found to the so-called British problem was not just because an imbalance between receipts and contributions existed but because it offended against the principles of fiscal equity. It did not seem reasonable that a country which, at least before the accession of Spain and Portugal, enjoyed a GNP below the Community average should make such a substantial contribution to the budget. It was therefore in the interest of the whole Community that a solution be found.

At the same time, the debate on the British question opened up a much broader discussion. If the British situation was unfair, what would a fair budget look like? Would it be one in which each country received precisely what it paid in? If not, then on the basis of what criteria should a fair budget be judged? These questions led back ineluctably to the issue of redistribution which was at the centre of the debate on economic and social cohesion. The incorporation of this idea in the Treaty through the SEA reflected an increased willingness on the part of the Community to assume a responsibility, in however rudimentary a form, for the well-being of the weaker economies within it. Moreover, the fulfilment of such a responsibility was seen to be possible only through a substantial injection of funds which would redistribute resources away from the richer to the poorer countries. To argue that the doubling of the funds was nothing more than the negotiated quid pro quo for the creation of the single market and that the need for structural spending will disappear once that market is in place would be to misunderstand the strength of the idea of cohesion. There is no doubt that, far from becoming less important, the redistributive function of the budget will be needed even more in future, unless one makes the very optimistic assumption that the gains from market integration will be distributed evenly.

This line of argument is not intended to suggest that the idea of a British abatement mechanism no longer makes sense. Rather it is designed to encourage the thought that its present form may no longer be appropriate. Although it was agreed at the Brussels European Council to maintain the Fontainebleau agreement more or less as it was, this is likely to prove a much more difficult task at the beginning of the nineties. By then the transitional mechanisms limiting the budgetary contributions of Spain and Portugal will have come to an end and structural spending, offering an alternative route to combating imbalance and emphasizing the redistributive principle, will be in full swing. A move away from the present revenue-side arrangement, which obliges all member states to contribute to the resolution of the British problem regardless of prosperity, to one on the expenditure-side will have to be reconsidered. As Padoa-Schioppa suggests, such an arrangement need not involve the expansion of Community policies specifically to benefit Britain but could be brought about by a safeguard mechanism which relates net balances to the income per head of countries and provides for corrective payments to or from the budget. The result would be 'to separate out the processes of shaping individual Community policies from concern over their income distribution consequences'.[4] In this way the particular interests of member states could be subsumed within a wider Community interest, designed to improve both the allocative and redistributive elements within the budget.

How much autonomy?
One of the difficulties with proposals like that just cited is that they lead logically to a budgetary procedure which enjoys a marked degree of autonomy from national interference and which explicitly recognizes certain principles established outside the national sphere that should guide the relations between the Community as a whole and its constituent parts. Such a movement is one which has generally been resisted in the Council and been at the root of many of the conflicts which have pitted it against the EP over the years. Traditionally, for example, the Parliament argued that entry in the budget constituted a sufficient legal base for the implementation of appropriations. The Council, for its part, took the view that the budget procedure was subordinate to the legislative process where it enjoyed the last word. A temporary truce was agreed in 1982 with the signing of a Joint Declaration which stated that 'the implementation of appropriations entered for significant new Community action shall require a basic regulation.'[5] However, this still left plenty of room for argument as to what actions are neither significant nor new and thus permit implementation without a legal base agreed in

Council. As a result, some in the Council, in particular Britain, have favoured getting rid of such flexibility altogether and obliging the Commission to obtain a legal base even for small-scale expenditure.

Once again the stress on national prerogatives and the reluctance to look at the Community budget more broadly may prove to be misleading in the longer term. The attempt to limit the budgetary discretion of the Commission looks like an increasingly irrelevant tactic as the Community moves into the 1990s. Perhaps it made sense from a national point of view in an earlier era when much more faith was placed in the value of public expenditure and its use in encouraging integration. However, the climate of opinion has changed radically since the appearance of the MacDougall report in 1977 with its vision of a 'small public sector federation', involving expenditure ranging between 5 and 10% of GDP. The Padoa-Schioppa report bears witness to a move towards a far less advanced role for Community spending, which the Brussels European Council endorsed.

In part, this can be explained by the fact that there is a far greater awareness that there can be 'a very strong Community government with a slender purse'.[6] Ludlow quotes the example of competition policy which provides scope for the Community, in the shape of the Commission, to exercise a substantial degree of control over national public expenditure. One could add that the same tendency is likely to develop as the Community moves more seriously towards joint economic management. The decision of the Council to agree a regulation providing medium-term financial support for any Member State in balance of payments difficulties is a case in point.[7] The regulation provides for aid in the form of loans up to a total of 14 billion ecus. This amount has no direct impact on the budget, although Article 830 in the budget does provide for an open-ended guarantee in the event of default. However, such loan provision is certain to alter the character of relations between the member states particularly after the liberalization of capital movements. Weaker currencies are likely to be increasingly vulnerable and to require more support than that at present available, something which the other states will be reluctant to agree to without imposing certain conditions. An IMF-type relationship between Community and debtor could develop with the difference that the loans would be within the family rather than at arms-length. The debates can be expected to be as difficult as they are critical in influencing domestic economic choices.

This movement towards a broader Community agenda has already had some effect on the way in which budgetary questions are looked at. The issue of implementation, for example, has encouraged a re-examination of the traditional dichotomy between state autonomy and Community competence. The debate on future financing that led up to the Brussels European Council revealed that a reinforcement of the capabilities of the Community institutions at the expense of national ones can be an attractive option for member states. Britain found itself on the side of the Commission when it came to seeking to ensure maximum rigour in the agricultural sector. As the journalist Quentin Peel pointed out in the *Financial Times*:

> Where the UK and the Commission are remarkably in tune is on giving the Commission much stronger management powers to control costs week by week. Almost all the rest are petrified of such loss of power to Brussels, but the British see it as the only way to give spending controls real teeth.[8]

This shows quite clearly how difficult it is to argue simply in terms of a bold contrast between a centralizing Europe and a Europe where member states cooperate. For member states to cooperate effectively they may themselves wish to accord certain wider powers to the centre.

Old issues revisited

If the Community agenda continues to widen, then it ought to be possible to pursue an approach less tainted by concerns about national sovereignty and to look afresh at certain issues which have dogged budgetary debates over the years. Is, for example, the distinction between compulsory and non-compulsory expenditure one that it is essential to maintain once there is broad agreement on the direction of Community spending? Such a consensus is not a foregone conclusion but the interinstitutional agreement offers the kind of framework within which the abolition of the distinction could be considered. By creating a new intermediate kind of expenditure referred to in Chapter 2 as 'compulsory non-compulsory', the Brussels European Council effectively undermined the old arguments about the maximum rate and the amounts by which the non-compulsory sector could increase. At the same time, it weakened the contention that compulsory spending was so special that it had unlimited claims on the budget. It would be foolish to deny that agricultural spending still has a particular resonance for some states but it is not clear that this cannot be respected by devices other than the CE/NCE distinction.

The same kind of reasoning can be applied to the issue of revenue. At the present time, any decision to increase revenue has to be recommended for adoption to the member states by the Council 'in accordance with their respective constitutional requirements' (Article 201 of the EEC Treaty). In other words, the decision is a national one and one where the Community institutions have a strictly limited role. This situation was not modified by the agreement made in Brussels. The decision on own resources had to be ratified by national parliaments and it includes the provision that 'revenue deriving from any new charges introduced within the framework of a common policy' (Article 2(2)) will have to be approved by the same procedure. In other words, a fifth resource cannot be agreed through the Community institutions, even if the revenue generated does not lead to the GNP ceilings being exceeded.

What is more, the agreement on a fourth resource has made it possible to expand the budget indefinitely without changing the components of the revenue system, or making them to any extent more *communautaire*. For many the new resource looks distinctly like a national contribution by another name and lacks any clearly defined status as a Community resource. It is salutary to recall in this context what the Commission itself said ten years ago when future financing was under discussion:

. . . it is important that the Community's system of financing should continue to develop towards true own resources. There can be no question of reverting to financial contributions from

71

member states. To do so would be contrary to the Treaty. It would, moreover, tend to focus attention on the already latent concern with *juste retour* in the member states and could make it more difficult to achieve progress towards the development of Community action.[9]

The arguments in favour of the status quo are powerful ones but it is worth presenting an alternative scenario which takes account of the fact that few now see the need for a massive rise in spending at EC level and many envisage the influence of the Community being exercised on a broader economic front. Under these circumstances the 'public goods' provided by the Community would increase and concern about narrower budgetary issues could be expected to decline. This in turn could open the way to a greater willingness to involve the Parliament in the determination of revenue. At present, it enjoys what has been called the 'luxury of revenue irresponsibility'.[10] In other words, it can increase expenditure within certain limits without being obliged to account for the corresponding increase in revenue. A recognition that the sums at stake were not so large might help to encourage governments to pursue further the path of 'responsibilizing' the Parliament.

It is not as if the idea of a tax-raising power at European level is so revolutionary. The European Coal and Steel Community, as mentioned in Chapter 1, has had such a power since 1952 and can apply a levy of up to 1% on products covered by the Treaty. Rather the difficulty is overcoming resistance to taxes, whose impact is very unlikely to be broadly neutral as between member states. The much-canvassed idea of a levy on oil imports, for example, would fall very unevenly on different states with countries like Italy that are heavily dependent on energy imports being particularly severely penalized.[11] However, there is no reason why a new tax should be neutral in its impact: after all, the existing sources of revenue are not. The question to decide is whether other policy objectives (such as energy conservation, in the case of the oil levy) make it worthwhile introducing such a tax at Community level. It will therefore be of considerable interest to see whether the Commission does introduce a proposal for a new form of Community taxation as it suggested it might in its report on future financing.[12]

These comments are intended to serve not as a prophecy of what will occur but rather as an encouragement to look at old questions in a new light as the role of the Community develops. In particular, it is surely no longer adequate to talk of a direct trade-off between state sovereignty and Community competence. The issue is not whether there should be some closer central coordination of policy. It concerns, instead, the areas in which that central coordination should take place and the nature of the powers to be exercised there. Moreover, such judgments cannot be made simply on the basis of individual interests but need to take account of a broader Community interest. The latter is not simply the sum of the former: the Community does exist to satisfy the wants of its members but it also represents a system of government with an intrinsic value of its own. The shape of that system was certainly influenced by the successful outcome of the Brussels European Council but it did not assume a definitive form. For this reason alone the debate on the budget will remain on the Community agenda.

ANNEXES

Annex I
Financial Provisions of the Treaty establishing the European Economic Community (Title II of Part Five)

Article 199

All items of revenue and expenditure of the Community, including those relating to the European Social Fund, shall be included in estimates to be drawn up for each financial year and shall be shown in the budget.

The revenue and expenditure shown in the budget shall be in balance.

Article 200

1. The budget revenue shall include, irrespective of any other revenue, financial contributions of Member States on the following scale:

Belgium	7.9
Germany	28
France	28
Italy	28
Luxembourg	0.2
Netherlands	7.9

2. The financial contributions of Member States to cover the expenditure of the European Social Fund, however, shall be determined on the following scale:

Belgium	8.8
Germany	32
France	32
Italy	20
Luxembourg	0.2
Netherlands	7

3. The scales may be modified by the Council, acting unanimously.

Article 201

The Commission shall examine the conditions under which the financial contributions of Member States provided for in Article 200 could be replaced by the Community's own resources, in particular by revenue accruing from the common customs tariff when it has been finally introduced.

To this end, the Commission shall submit proposals to the Council.

After consulting the European Parliament on these proposals the Council may, acting unanimously, lay down the appropriate provisions, which it shall recommend to the Member States for adoption in accordance with their respective constitutional requirements.

Article 202

The expenditure shown in the budget shall be authorized for one financial year, unless the regulations made pursuant to Article 209 provide otherwise.

In accordance with conditions to be laid down pursuant to Article 209, any appropriations, other than those relating to staff expenditure, that are unexpended at the end of the financial year may be carried forward to the next financial year only.

Appropriations shall be classified under different chapters grouping items of expenditure according to their nature or purpose and subdivided, as far as may be necessary, in accordance with the regulations made pursuant to Article 209.

The expenditure of the European Parliament, the Council, the Commission and the Court of Justice shall be set out in separate parts of the budget, without prejudice to special arrangements for certain common items of expenditure.

Article 203

1. The financial year shall run from 1 January to 31 December.
2. Each institution of the Community shall, before 1 July, draw up

estimates of its expenditure. The Commission shall consolidate these estimates in a preliminary draft budget. It shall attach thereto an opinion which may contain different estimates.

The preliminary draft budget shall contain an estimate of revenue and an estimate of expenditure.

3. The Commission shall place the preliminary draft budget before the Council not later than 1 September of the year preceding that in which the budget is to be implemented.

The Council shall consult the Commission and, where appropriate, the other institutions concerned whenever it intends to depart from the preliminary draft budget.

The Council, acting by a qualified majority, shall establish the draft budget and forward it to the European Parliament.

4. The draft budget shall be placed before the European Parliament not later than 5 October of the year preceding that in which the budget is to be implemented.

The European Parliament shall have the right to amend the draft budget, acting by a majority of its members, and to propose to the Council, acting by an absolute majority of the votes cast, modifications to the draft budget relating to expenditure necessarily resulting from this Treaty or from acts adopted in accordance therewith.

If, within 45 days of the draft budget being placed before it, the European Parliament has given its approval, the budget shall stand as finally adopted. If within this period the European Parliament has not amended the draft budget nor proposed any modifications thereto, the budget shall be deemed to be finally adopted.

If within this period the European Parliament has adopted amendments or proposed modifications, the draft budget together with the amendments or proposed modifications shall be forwarded to the Council.

5. After discussing the draft budget with the Commission and, where appropriate, with the other institutions concerned, the Council shall act under the following conditions:

(a) The Council may, acting by a qualified majority, modify any of the amendments adopted by the European Parliament;

(b) With regard to the proposed modifications:

– where a modification proposed by the European Parliament does not have the effect of increasing the total amount of the expenditure of an institution, owing in particular to the fact that the increase in expenditure which it would involve would be expressly compensated by one or more proposed modifications correspondingly reducing expenditure, the Council may, acting by a qualified majority, reject the proposed modification. In the absence of a decision to reject it, the proposed modifications shall stand as accepted;

– where a modification proposed by the European Parliament has the effect of increasing the total amount of the expenditure of an institution, the Council may, acting by a qualified majority, accept this proposed modification. In the absence of a decision to accept it, the proposed modification shall stand as rejected;

– where, in pursuance of one of the two preceding subparagraphs, the Council has rejected a proposed modification, it may, acting by a qualified majority, either retain the amount shown in the draft budget or fix another amount.

The draft budget shall be modified on the basis of the proposed modifications accepted by the Council.

If, within 15 days of the draft being placed before it, the Council has not modified any of the amendments adopted by the European Parliament and if the modifications proposed by the latter have been accepted, the budget shall be deemed to be finally adopted. The Council shall inform the European Parliament that it has not modified any of the amendments and that the proposed modifications have been accepted.

If within this period the Council has modified one or more of the amendments adopted by the European Parliament or if the modifications proposed by the latter have been rejected or modified, the modified draft budget shall again be forwarded to the European Parliament. The Council shall inform the European Parliament of the results of its deliberations.

6.   Within 15 days of the draft budget being placed before it, the European Parliament, which shall have been notified of the action taken on its proposed modifications, may, acting by a majority of its members and three-fifths of the votes cast, amend or reject the modifications to its amendments made by the Council and shall adopt the budget accordingly. If within this period the European Parliament has not acted, the budget shall be deemed to be finally adopted.

7.   When the procedure provided for in this Article has been completed, the President of the European Parliament shall declare that the budget has been finally adopted.

8.   However, the European Parliament, acting by a majority of its members

and two-thirds of the votes cast, may, if there are important reasons, reject the draft budget and ask for a new draft to be submitted to it.

9.   A maximum rate of increase in relation to the expenditure of the same type to be incurred during the current year shall be fixed annually for the total expenditure other than that necessarily resulting from this Treaty or from acts adopted in accordance therewith.

The Commission shall, after consulting the Economic Policy Committee, declare what this maximum rate is as it results from:

– the trend, in terms of volume, of the gross national product within the Community;

– the average variation in the budgets of the Member States;

and

– the trend of the cost of living during the preceding financial year.

The maximum rate shall be communicated before 1 May, to all the institutions of the Community. The latter shall be required to conform to this during the budgetary procedure, subject to the provisions of the fourth and fifth subparagraphs of this paragraph.

If, in respect of expenditure other than that necessarily resulting from this Treaty or from acts adopted in accordance therewith, the actual rate of increase in the draft budget established by the Council is over half the maximum rate, the European Parliament may, exercising its right of amendment, further increase the total amount of that expenditure to a limit not exceeding half the maximum rate.

Where the European Parliament, the Council or the Commission consider that the activities of the Communities require that the rate determined according to the procedure laid down in this paragraph should be exceeded, another rate may be fixed by agreement between the Council, acting by a qualified majority, and the European Parliament acting by a majority of its members and three-fifths of the votes cast.

10.   Each institution shall exercise the powers conferred upon it by this Article, with due regard for the provisions of the Treaty and for acts adopted in accordance therewith, in particular those relating to the Communities' own resources and to the balance between revenue and expenditure.

79

Article 204

If at the beginning of a financial year, the budget has not yet been voted, a sum equivalent to not more than one-twelfth of the budget appropriations for the preceding financial year may be spent each month in respect of any chapter or other subdivision of the budget in accordance with the provisions of the Regulations made pursuant to Article 209; this arrangement shall not, however, have the effect of placing at the disposal of the Commission appropriations in excess of one-twelfth of those provided for in the draft budget in course of preparation.

The Council may, acting by a qualified majority, provided that the other conditions laid down in the first subparagraph are observed, authorize expenditure in excess of one-twelfth.

If the decision relates to expenditure which does not necessarily result from this Treaty or from acts adopted in accordance therewith, the Council shall forward it immediately to the European Parliament; within 30 days the European Parliament, acting by a majority of its members and three-fifths of the votes cast, may adopt a different decision on the expenditure in excess of the one-twelfth referred to in the first subparagraph. This part of the decision of the Council shall be suspended until the European Parliament has taken its decision. If within the said period the European Parliament has not taken a decision which differs from the decision of the Council, the latter shall be deemed to be finally adopted.

The decisions referred to in the second and third subparagraphs shall lay down the necessary measures relating to resources to ensure application of this Article.

Article 205

The Commission shall implement the budget, in accordance with provisions of the regulations made pursuant to Article 209, on its own responsibility and within the limits of the appropriations.

The regulations shall lay down detailed rules for each institution concerning its part in effecting its own expenditure.

Within the budget, the Commission may, subject to the limits and conditions laid down in the regulations made pursuant to Article 209, transfer appropriations from one chapter to another or from one subdivision to another.

Article 205a

The Commission shall submit annually to the Council and to the European Parliament the accounts of the preceding financial year relating to the implementation of the budget. The Commission shall also forward to them a financial statement of the assets and liabilities of the Community.

Article 206

1. A Court of Auditors is hereby established.
2. The Court of Auditors shall consist of twelve members.
3. The members of the Court of Auditors shall be chosen from among persons who belong or have belonged in their respective countries to external audit bodies or who are especially qualified for this office. Their independence must be beyond doubt.
4. The members of the Court of Auditors shall be appointed for a term of six years by the Council, acting unanimously after consulting the European Parliament.

However, when the first appointments are made, four members of the Court of Auditors, chosen by lot, shall be appointed for a term of office of four years only.

The members of the Court of Auditors shall be eligible for reappointment.

They shall elect the President of the Court of Auditors from among their number for a term of three years. The President may be re-elected.

5. The members of the Court of Auditors shall, in the general interest of the Community, be completely independent in the performance of their duties.

In the performance of these duties, they shall neither seek nor take instructions from any government or from any other body. They shall refrain from any action incompatible with their duties.

6. The members of the Court of Auditors may not, during their term of office, engage in any other occupation, whether gainful or not. When entering upon their duties they shall give a solemn undertaking that, both during and after their term of office, they will respect the obligations arising therefrom and in particular their duty to behave with integrity and discretion as regards the acceptance, after they have ceased to hold office, of certain appointments or benefits.

7. Apart from normal replacement, or death, the duties of a member of the Court of Auditors shall end when he resigns, or is compulsorily retired by a ruling of the Court of Justice pursuant to paragraph 8.

The vacancy thus caused shall be filled for the remainder of the member's term of office.

Save in the case of compulsory retirement, members of the Court of Auditors shall remain in office until they have been replaced.

8.   A member of the Court of Auditors may be deprived of his office or of his right to a pension or other benefits in its stead only if the Court of Justice, at the request of the Court of Auditors, finds that he no longer fulfils the requisite conditions or meets the obligations arising from his office.

9.   The Council, acting by a qualified majority, shall determine the conditions of employment of the President and the members of the Court of Auditors and in particular their salaries, allowances and pensions. It shall also, by the same majority, determine any payment to be made instead of remuneration.

10.   The provisions of the Protocol on the Privileges and Immunities of the European Communities applicable to the Judges of the Court of Justice shall also apply to the members of the Court of Auditors.

Article 206a

1.   The Court of Auditors shall examine the accounts of all revenue and expenditure of the Community. It shall also examine the accounts of all revenue and expenditure of all bodies set up by the Community in so far as the relevant constituent instrument does not preclude such examination.

2.   The Court of Auditors shall examine whether all revenue has been received and all expenditure incurred in a lawful and regular manner and whether the financial management has been sound.

The audit of revenue shall be carried out on the basis both of the amounts established as due and the amounts actually paid to the Community.

The audit of expenditure shall be carried out on the basis both of commitments undertaken and payments made.

These audits may be carried out before the closure of accounts for the financial year in question.

3.   The audit shall be based on records and, if necessary, performed on the spot in the institutions of the Community and in the Member States. In the Member States the audit shall be carried out in liaison with the national audit bodies or, if these do not have the necessary powers, with the competent national departments. These bodies or departments shall inform the Court of Auditors whether they intend to take part in the audit.

The institutions of the Community and the national audit bodies or, if these do not have the necessary powers, the competent national departments, shall forward to the Court of Auditors, at its request, any document or information necessary to carry out its task.

4.   The Court of Auditors shall draw up an annual report after the close of each financial year. It shall be forwarded to the institutions of the Community and shall be published, together with the replies of these institutions to the observations of the Court of Auditors, in the *Official Journal of the European Communities*.

The Court of Auditors may also, at any time, submit observations on specific questions and deliver opinions at the request of one of the institutions of the Community.

It shall adopt its annual reports or opinions by a majority of its members.

It shall assist the European Parliament and the Council in exercising their powers of control over the implementation of the budget.

Article 206b

The European Parliament, acting on a recommendation from the Council which shall act by a qualified majority, shall give a discharge to the Commission in respect of the implementation of the budget. To this end, the Council and the European Parliament in turn shall examine the accounts and the financial statement referred to in Article 205a and the annual report by the Court of Auditors together with the replies of the institutions under audit to the observations of the Court of Auditors.

Article 207

The budget shall be drawn up in the unit of account determined in accordance with the provisions of the regulations made pursuant to Article 209.

The financial contributions provided for in Article 200 (1) shall be placed at the disposal of the Community by the Member States in their national currencies.

The available balances of these contributions shall be deposited with the Treasuries of Member States or with bodies designated by them. While on deposit, such funds shall retain the value corresponding to the parity, at the date of deposit, in relation to the unit of account referred to in the first paragraph.

The balances may be invested on terms to be agreed between the Commission and the Member State concerned.

The regulations made pursuant to Article 209 shall lay down the technical conditions under which financial operations relating to the European Social Fund shall be carried out.

Article 208

The Commission may, provided it notifies the competent authorities of the Member States concerned, transfer into the currency of one of the Member States its holdings in the currency of another Member State, to the extent necessary to enable them to be used for purposes which come within the scope of this Treaty. The Commission shall as far as possible avoid making such transfers if it possesses cash or liquid assets in the currencies which it needs.

The Commission shall deal with each Member State through the authority designated by the State concerned. In carrying out financial operations the Commission shall employ the services of the bank of issue of the Member State concerned or of any other financial institution approved by that State.

Article 209

The Council, acting unanimously on a proposal from the Commission and after consulting the European Parliament and obtaining the opinion of the Court of Auditors, shall:

(a) make Financial Regulations specifying in particular the procedure to be adopted for establishing and implementing the budget and for presenting and auditing accounts;

(b) determine the methods and procedure whereby the budget revenue provided under the arrangements relating to the Communities' own resources shall be made available to the Commission, and determine the measures to be applied, if need be, to meet cash requirements;

(c) lay down rules concerning the responsibility of authorizing officers and accounting officers and concerning appropriate arrangements for inspection.

Annex II
Council Decision of 24 June 1988
concerning budgetary discipline
(88/377/EEC)

THE COUNCIL OF THE EUROPEAN COMMUNITIES,

Having regard to the Treaty establishing the European Economic Community, and in particular Articles 43, 126, 127, 130d, 130i, 203, 209 and 235 thereof,

Having regard to the proposal from the Commission,

Having regard to the opinion of the European Parliament,

Having regard to the opinion of the Court of Auditors,

Whereas at its meetings in Brussels in 1987 and 1988 the European Council agreed to submit the use of the Community's own resources to effective and legally binding discipline parallel to the efforts being made by the Member States in connection with their own budgets; whereas that discipline must be strengthened in the light of experience on the basis of the arrangements adopted by the European Council at Fontainebleau;

Whereas, in addition, an agreement, hereinafter referred to as the 'Interinstitutional Agreement', was reached between the European Parliament, the Council and the Commission with the aim of attaining the objectives of the Single European Act, of putting in concrete form the conclusions reached by the European Council at the said meetings on budgetary discipline and of improving the operation of the annual budgetary procedure and whereas it will take effect on 1 July 1988;

Whereas budgetary discipline must be applied to all the Community's expenditure and whereas it must cover both payment and commitment appropriations;

Whereas on 11 to 13 February 1988 the European Council agreed upon the principles of a guideline for the control of agricultural expenditure (hereinafter referred to as the 'agricultural guideline');

Whereas the rate of the European Agricultural Guidance and Guarantee Fund Guarantee expenditure must not exceed 74% of the rate of increase in Community gross national product, this rate corresponding to that of 80% if maximum EAGGF financing of set-aside were to be taken into consideration;

Whereas the European Council has also agreed to mechanisms for the systematic depreciation of existing and future agricultural stocks so that the stock situation can be normalized by 1992;

Whereas the stabilization mechanisms provided for in the provisions governing the common organization of markets should play a part in ensuring compliance with the agricultural guideline;

Whereas the European Council has also agreed that the level of EAGGF Guarantee expenditure may be influenced by movements in the dollar/ecu market rate and whereas, to cover development caused by significant and unforeseen movements in the dollar/ecu market rate compared to the rate used in the budget, a monetary reserve of ECU 1,000 million shall be entered each year in the budget in the form of provisional appropriations;

Whereas it is necessary that compulsory expenditure other than EAGGF Guarantee expenditure be subject to budgetary rigour and planning,

HAS ADOPTED THIS DECISION:

EAGGF Guarantee expenditure
Article 1

The rate of increase in EAGGF Guarantee expenditure – as defined in Article 3 – between 1988 and a given year must not exceed 74% of the rate of increase in Community gross national product during the same period.

The maximum progression for EAGGF Guarantee expenditure (the agricultural guideline), which would correspond to 80% if maximum EAGGF financing of set-aside were taken into consideration, must be respected each year.

Article 2

The 1988 base of expenditure from which the agricultural guideline for each subsequent year is to be calculated shall be ECU 27,500 million, to be adjusted according to Article 3. The statistical base with regard to GNP statistics shall correspond to that used in Council Decision 88/376/EEC, Euratom of 24 June 1988 on the system of the Communities' own resources. All calculations which shall be made by the Commission at the time of submitting its annual price-fixing proposal, subject to a possible final review at the time of submitting the preliminary draft budget for the following year, shall be established in 1988 prices and converted into current prices by use of the GNP deflator estimated by the Commission for the year in question.

Article 3
The expenditure to which Article 1 applies shall be the expenditure chargeable to Section III, Part B, Titles 1 and 2 (EAGGF Guarantee) of the budget, including expenditure relating to set-aside within a maximum annual amount which may not exceed ECU 150 million (1988 prices) up to 1992, less amounts corresponding to the disposal of ACP sugar food aid refunds, sugar and isoglucose levy payments by producers and any other revenue raised from the agricultural sector in the future.

Article 4
The agricultural guideline shall include costs relating to depreciation of newly created agricultural stocks. Each year the Council shall enter in its draft budget the appropriations necessary for financing all costs relating to depreciation of new stocks. The appropriations shall be used for the systematic depreciation of the new stocks, which shall start when these are formed, in accordance with the provisions which will be inserted in Council Regulation (EEC) No 1883/78 of 2 August 1978 laying down general rules for the financing of interventions by the European Agricultural Guidance and Guarantee Section as last amended by Regulation (EEC) No 2050/88.

The cost of depreciating existing surplus agricultural stocks shall be met outside the agricultural guideline. The following amounts shall be included in Title 8 of the budget for the period 1988 to 1992 (1988 prices):

1988:	ECU 1 200 million,
1989–92:	ECU 1 400 million.

These amounts may not be used for any other purposes.

The procedures for the financial compensation granted to Spain and Portugal in respect of their contribution to the financing of these stocks shall be dealt with by Regulation (EEC) No 2051/88. These two Member States shall be treated as if the depreciation of stocks had been entirely financed by the Community in 1987.

87

Article 5

The Commission's price proposals shall be consistent with the limits laid down by the agricultural guideline.

If the Commission considers that the outcome of the Council's discussions on these price proposals is likely to exceed the costs put forward in its original proposal, the final decision shall be referred to a special meeting of the Council.

The agricultural guideline must be respected each year.

Article 6

To ensure that the agricultural guideline is respected, the Commission shall establish an 'early warning system' covering the development of expenditure of the individual EAGGF Guarantee expenditure chapters. Before the beginning of each budget year the Commission shall define expenditure profiles for each EAGGF Guarantee budget chapter based on the monthly expenditure over the three preceding years. The Commission shall submit monthly reports thereafter to the European Parliament and the Council on the development of actual expenditure against profiles. Where the rate of development of expenditure is exceeding the forecast profile, or risks doing so, the Commission shall use the management powers at its disposal, including those which it has under the stabilizing measures, to remedy the situation. If these measures are insufficient, the Commission shall examine the functioning of the agricultural stabilizers in the relevant sector and, if necessary, shall present proposals to the Council calculated to strengthen their action. The Council shall act within a period of two months in order to remedy the situation.

Article 7

Payment of the monthly EAGGF Guarantee advances by the Commission shall be effected on the basis of the information supplied by the Member States in regard to agricultural expenditure for each common market organization.

Article 8

Where no appropriations are available, the Commission shall propose transfers to the budget authority.

Article 9

The dollar/ecu rate used to draw up the annual budget estimates of EAGGF Guarantee expenditure for any given year shall be the average market rate over the first three months of the preceding year. However, the rate used in the budget for 1988 shall be USD 1 = ECU 0.85.

Article 10

ECU 1,000 million shall be included annually in a reserve of the general budget of the European Communities, as a provision for covering developments caused by significant and unforeseen movements in the dollar/ecu market rate compared to the dollar/ecu rate used in the budget. These appropriations shall be included in the agricultural guideline.

Article 11

Each October, the Commission shall report to the budget authority on the impact on EAGGF Guarantee expenditure of movements in the average dollar/ecu market rate for the period 1 August of the preceding year to 31 July of the current year compared to the rate used in the budget, as defined in Article 9.

Article 12

Savings or additional costs resulting from movements in the rate shall be treated in a symmetrical fashion. Where the dollar strengthens against the ecu compared to the rate used in the budget, savings in the Guarantee Section of up to ECU 1,000 million shall be transferred to the monetary reserve. Where additional budgetary costs are engendered by a fall in the dollar against the ecu compared with the budget rate, the monetary reserve shall be called up and transfers shall be made from the monetary reserve to the EAGGF Guarantee Section lines affected by the fall in the dollar. The necessary own resources shall be called up, in accordance with Decision 88/376/EEC, Euratom and the provisions adopted pursuant thereto, to finance the corresponding expenditure.

Any savings made in the EAGGF Guarantee Section which have been transferred to the monetary reserve in accordance with the first sub-paragraph and which remain in the monetary reserve shall be cancelled and thus contribute to a budgetary surplus which shall be counted as a revenue item in succeeding budgets. This shall be done by means of a letter of amendment during the budgetary procedure concerning the budget for the coming year.

Article 13

There shall be a franchise of ECU 400 million. Savings or additional costs below this amount will not necessitate transfers to or from the monetary reserve. Savings or additional costs above this amount shall be paid into, or met from, the monetary reserve.

Article 14

Each year, at the start of the budget procedure, the Council shall adopt a reference framework, taking account of the financial estimates of the Interinstitutional Agreement, for compulsory expenditure other than EAGGF Guarantee expenditure. The reference framework shall include the maximum amounts for both commitment and payment appropriations which the Council considers necessary with due regard for the Community's legal obligations.

Non-compulsory expenditure
Article 15

The budgetary discipline applicable to non-compulsory expenditure shall be ensured on the basis of the arrangements contained in the Interinstitutional Agreement.

Other provisions
Article 16

The financial implementation of any Council Decision exceeding the budget appropriations available in the general budget or the appropriations provided for in the financial estimates may not take place until the budget and, where appropriate, the financial estimates have been suitably amended according to the procedure laid down for each of these cases.

Article 17

The Decision shall remain in force for the duration of Decision 88/376/EEC, Euratom.

Article 18

This Decision is addressed to the Member States.

Done at Luxembourg, 24 June 1988.

For the Council
The President
M. BANGEMANN

Annex III
Interinstitutional Agreement on budgetary discipline and improvement of the budgetary procedure (Official Journal No L 185 of 15 July 1988)

I. BASIC PRINCIPLES OF THE AGREEMENT

1. The main purpose of the Interinstitutional Agreement is to achieve the objectives of the Single European Act, to give effect to the conclusions of the Brussels European Council on budgetary discipline and accordingly to improve the functioning of the annual budgetary procedure.

2. Budgetary discipline under the Interinstitutional Agreement covers all expenditure and is binding on all the institutions involved for as long as the Agreement is in force.

3. This Agreement does not alter the respective budgetary powers of the various institutions as laid down in the Treaty.

4. The contents of the Interinstitutional Agreement may not be changed without the consent of all the institutions which are party to it.

II. BUDGET FORECASTS: FINANCIAL PERSPECTIVE 1988 to 1992

A. Contents

5. The financial perspective 1988 to 1992 constitutes the reference framework for interinstitutionl budgetary discipline. Its contents are consistent with the conclusions of the Brussels European Council; it forms an integral part of the Agreement.

6. The financial perspective 1988 to 1992 indicates, in commitments appropriations, the volume and breakdown of foreseeable Community expenditure, including that for the development of new policies.

B. Nature

7. The European Parliament, the Council and the Commission recognize that each of the financial objectives laid down in the perspective 1988 to 1992 represents an annual expenditure ceiling for the Community. They undertake to observe the different ceilings during the corresponding budgetary procedure.

8. The European Parliament, the Council and the Commission will join in the effort undertaken by the Community gradually to achieve a better balance between the various categories of expenditure.

They give an undertaking that any revision of the compulsory expenditure figure given in the financial perspective will not cause the amount of non-compulsory expenditure shown in the perspective to be reduced.

C. Annual adjustment

– Technical adjustments

9. Each year, the Commission will update the perspective ahead of the budgetary procedure for year t + 1, making technical adjustments to the figures in line with movements in gross national product (GNP) and prices.

– Adjustments connected with the conditions for implementation

10. When notifying the two arms of the budgetary authority of the technical adjustments to the financial perspective, the Commission will present any proposals for adjustments it considers necessary to take account of the conditions for implementation on the basis of the schedules of utilization of commitment appropriations and payment appropriations.

The European Parliament and the Council will take decisions on these proposals, before 1 May of year t, in accordance with the majority rules specified in Article 203(9) of the Treaty.

11. If the allocations provided in the financial perspective for multiannual programmes cannot be used in full during a given year, the institutions party to the Agreement undertake to authorize the transfer of the remaining allocations.

D. Revision

12. In addition to the regular technical adjustments and adjustments in line with the conditions for implementation, the financial perspective may be revised by a joint decision of the two arms of the budgetary authority, acting on a proposal from the Commission.

The joint decision will be taken in accordance with the majority rules specified in Article 203(9) of the Treaty.

The revision of the financial perspective may not raise the overall expenditure ceiling, as set by this perspective after the annual technical adjustment, above a margin for unforeseen expenditure of 0.03% of GNP. It must also respect the provisions of point 8 of this Interinstitutional Agreement.

E. Consequences of the absence of a joint decision by the institutions on the adjustment or revision of the financial perspective

13. In the absence of a joint decision by the institutions on any adjustment or revision of the financial perspective proposed by the Commission the financial objectives already determined will, after the annual technical adjustment, remain applicable as the expenditure ceilings for the financial year in question.

III. BUDGETARY DISCIPLINE FOR COMPULSORY EXPENDITURE

14. (a) The European Parliament, the Council and the Commission are in agreement on the conclusions of the European Council concerning budgetary discipline for compulsory expenditure in the EAGGF Guarantee Section.

The three institutions undertake, within this Agreement, to respect these conclusions.

(b) The European Parliament, the Council and the Commission confirm the principles and the mechanisms for the agricultural guideline and the monetary reserve.

(c) As regards the other compulsory expenditure, the three institutions undertake to honour the Community's legal obligations in a manner consistent with the financial perspective.

IV. BUDGETARY DISCIPLINE FOR NON-COMPULSORY EXPENDITURE AND IMPROVEMENT OF THE BUDGETARY PROCEDURE

15. The two arms of the budgetary authority agree to accept, for the financial years 1988 to 1992, the maximum rates of increase for non-compulsory expenditure deriving from the budgets established within the ceilings set by the financial perspective.

16. The Commission will present each year, within the limits of the financial perspective, a preliminary draft budget based on the Community's actual financing requirements.

It will take into account:

- the capacity for utilizing appropriations, endeavouring to maintain a strict relationship between commitment appropriations and payment appropriations;

- the possibilities for starting up new policies or continuing multiannual operations which are coming to an end, after assessing whether it will be possible to secure a proper legal base.

17. Within the maximum rates of increase for non-compulsory expenditure specified in paragraph 15 of this Agreement, the European Parliament and the Council undertake to respect the allocations of commitment appropriations provided in the financial perspective for the Structural Funds, the Specific Industrial Development Programme for Portugal (PEDIP), the Integrated Mediterranean Programmes (IMPs) and the Research-Technology-Development (RTD) framework programme.

They also undertake to bear in mind the assessment of the possibilities for executing the budget made by the Commission in its preliminary drafts.

V. EQUIVALENCE BETWEEN ANNUAL EXPENDITURE CEILINGS AND ANNUAL CEILINGS FOR CALLING IN COMMUNITY OWN RESOURCES

18. The three institutions party to the Agreement agree that the overall expenditure ceiling for each year also represents the annual own resources call-in ceiling for the corresponding budget year. This will be expressed as a percentage of Community GNP.

VI. FINAL PROVISIONS

19.   This Interinstitutional Agreement for 1988 to 1992 will enter into force on 1 July 1988.

Before the end of 1991 the Commission will present a report on the application of this Agreement and on the amendments which need to be made to it in the light of experience.

Financial perspective
commitment appropriations in million ecus at 1988 prices

	1988	1989	1990	1991	1992
1. Guarantee Section of the EAGGF	**27,500**	**27,700**	**28,400**	**29,000**	**29,000**
2. Structural operations	**7,790**	**9,200**	**10,600**	**12,100**	**13,450**
3. Policies with multi-annual allocations (IMPs, research)*	**1,210**	**1,650**	**1,900**	**2,150**	**2,400**
4. Other policies	**2,103**	**2,385**	**2,500**	**2,700**	**2,800**
of which: NCE	1,646	1,801	1,860	1,910	1,970
5. Repayments and administration	**5,700**	**4,950**	**4,500**	**4,000**	**3,550**
of which: financing of stock disposal	1,240	1,400	1,400	1,400	1,400
6. Monetary reserve**	**1,000**	**1,000**	**1,000**	**1,000**	**1,000**
Total	**45,303**	**46,885**	**48,900**	**50,950**	**52,800**
of which†:					
— CE	33,698	32,607	32,810	32,980	33,400
— NCE	11,605	14,278	16,090	17,970	19,400
Payment appropriations required	**43,779**	**45,300**	**46,900**	**48,600**	**50,100**
of which†:					
— CE	33,640	32,604	32,740	32,910	33,110
— NCE	10,139	12,696	14,160	15,690	16,990
Payment appropriations as % of GNP	**1.12%**	**1.14%**	**1.15%**	**1.16%**	**1.17%**
Margin for unforeseen expenditure	**0.03%**	**0.03%**	**0.03%**	**0.03%**	**0.03%**
Own resources as % of GNP	**1.15%**	**1.17%**	**1.18%**	**1.19%**	**1.20%**

Notes:
* Chapter F on budget estimates of the European Council indicates a figure of 2,400 million [ecus] (1988 prices) for policies with multiannual allocations in 1992. The policies in question are R&D and IMPs. Only expenditure for which a legal basis exists may be financed under this heading. The present framework programme provides a legal basis for Research expenditure of 863 million ecus (current prices) for 1992. The regulation on IMPs provides a legal basis for an estimated amount of 300 million ecus in 1992 (current prices). The two arms of the Budgetary Authority undertake to respect the principle that further budget appropriations within this ceiling for 1990, 1991 and 1992 will require a revision of the existing framework programme or, before the end of 1991, a decision on a new framework programme based on a proposal from the Commission in accordance with the legislative provisions in Article 130Q of the SEA.
** At current prices.
† Based on the classification proposed by the Commission in the 1989 preliminary draft budget. The required decision by the budgetary authority will be implemented as a technical adjustment, under point 9 of the agreement.

Annex IV
Financial perspective as adapted in April 1989
commitment appropriations in million ecus

	1988*	1989*	1990**	1991**	1992**
1. Guarantee Section of the EAGGF	**27,500**	**28,613**	**30,700**	**31,350**	**32,000**
2. Structural operations	**7,790**	**9,522**	**11,555**	**13,160**	**14,630**
3. Policies with multi-annual allocations (IMPs, research)	**1,210**	**1,708**	**2,071**	**2,340**	**2,610**
4. Other policies	**2,103**	**2,468**	**2,729**	**2,940**	**3,050**
of which: NCE	1,646	1,864	2,023	2,080	2,140
5. Repayments and administration	**5,741**	**5,153**	**4,930**	**4,390**	**3,900**
of which: financing of stock disposal	1,240	1,449	1,523	1,523	1,523
6. Monetary reserve	**1,000**	**1,000**	**1,000**	**1,000**	**1,000**
Total	**45,344**	**48,464**	**52,985**	**55,180**	**57,190**
of which†:					
— CE	33,739	33,764	35,454	35,630	36,080
— NCE	11,605	14,700	17,531	19,550	21,110
Payment appropriations required	**43,820**	**46,885**	**50,791**	**56,620**	**54,250**
of which†:					
— CE	33,681	33,745	35,372	35,550	35,770
— NCE	10,139	13,140	15,419	17,070	18,480
Payment appropriations as % of GNP	**1.11%**	**1.10%**	**1.12%**	**1.13%**	**1.13%**
Margin for unforeseen expenditure	**0.03%**	**0.03%**	**0.03%**	**0.03%**	**0.03%**
Own resources as % of GNP	**1.14%**	**1.13%**	**1.15%**	**1.16%**	**1.16%**

Notes:
The table above shows the financial perspective of the June 1988 Interinstitutional Agreement after the annual adjustment adopted by Parliament and the Council in April 1989 on the basis of a Commission proposal.
* Current prices
** Constant prices.
The three footnotes in the original version of the perspective were not modified at the time of the 1989 adjustment.

NOTES

Chapter 2

1 Centre for European Policy Studies (1986), *The Future of Community Finance* (prepared by L. Spaventa, L. Koopmans, P. Salmon, B. Spahn and S. Smith), p. 13.

2 Commission of the European Communities (1987), *Report by the Commission to the Council and Parliament on the Financing of the Community Budget* (COM(87)101 final), p. 6.

3 88/376/EEC, Euratom (OJ L 185 of 15 July 1988, p. 24).

4 Ibid., Articles 2 and 4.

5 Council Decision 70/244/ECSC, EEC, Euratom in OJ L 94 of 28 April 1970.

6 Commission of the European Communities, Report cited in note 2, above, p. 16.

7 Ibid., p. 13.

8 Conclusions of the European Council of 11/12 February 1988, Chapter A, para. 14.

9 In the financial perspective, category 2 'Structural operations' contains finance for set-aside, income support and the programme for the development of Portuguese industry. Hence the discrepancy between figures in the perspective and those in the text here.

Chapter 3

1 Draft General Budget of the European Communities for the

Financial Year 1989 established by the Council, Volume VII, Council explanatory memorandum, p. 13.

2   Commission of the European Communities (1989), Preliminary Draft General Budget of the European Communities for the Financial Year 1990, Overview, (COM(89)175).

3   Ibid., p. 24.

4   1988 Brussels European Council Conclusions, Chapter A, para. 9.

5   Annual Report of the Court of Auditors for 1987, OJ C 316 of 12 December 1988, p. 221.

6   W. Nicoll (1988), 'L'accord interinstitutionnel sur la discipline budgétaire et l'amélioration de la procédure budgétaire' in *Revue du Marché Commun*, no. 319, July-August 1988, p. 376.

7   Article 1(3) of Council Regulation No. 2049/88 amending the Financial Regulation of 21 December 1977.

8   Article 21(3) of Regulation No. 4253/88.

Chapter 4

1   In the negotiations on the revision of the Financial Regulation that took place in 1989 the British government did persuade the Council to add the principle of cost-effectiveness to those of economy and sound financial management laid down in Article 2 governing the use of budget appropriations.

2   Annual Report of the Court of Auditors for 1987, OJ C 316 of 12 December 1988, p. 221.

3   Ibid., para. 4.55.

4   House of Lords, Session 1988–9, 5th Report of the Select Committee on the European Communities, *Fraud against the Community*, 21 February 1989.

5   Commission of the European Communities (1989), *Action Taken to Combat Fraud*, SEC (89) 1013.

6   Commission of the European Communities (COM(88)563 final), Seventeenth Financial Report on the EAGGF, 1987, Guarantee Section and Food Aid, Annex 22, p. 128.

7   Ibid., p. 46.

8   House of Lords, op. cit. in note 4, above, para. 145, p. 31.

9   Article 18(3) of Council Regulation No. 1552/89 of 29 May 1989 implementing Decision 88/376/EEC, Euratom on the system of the Communities' own resources, OJ L 155 of 7 June 1989.

10 House of Lords, Session 1987–8, Select Committee on the European

Communities, 14th Report, HL Paper 82, Reform of the Structural Funds, p. 108.

11 Ibid., p. 17 (para. 53 of the Conclusions).

12 Namely: (1) promoting the development of the less-developed regions; (2) assisting areas in industrial decline; (3) combating long-term unemployment; (4) facilitating occupational integration; and (5) promoting adjustment and development of rural areas.

13 The background to the whole question was thrown into sharp relief by the headline 'Europe's guilty secret' which appeared in the *Observer* of 10 September 1989. There followed a harrowing account of conditions for the mentally ill on the island of Leros and of some of the reasons why they had not been changed, despite the availability of Community funds.

14 Court of Auditors Special Report No 2/88 on the integrated approach to Community financing of structural measures, OJ C 188 of 18 July 1988.

15 Centre for European Policy Studies, *The Future of Community Finance*, p. 42.

Chapter 5

1 See Annex to the Minutes of 22 May 1989 of the European Parliament.

2 Dankert report drawn up on behalf of the Committee on Budgets (A 2–116/88), para. 17 of the explanatory statement.

3 Article 10 of the Council Decision on the system of the Communities' own resources (88/376/EEC, Euratom).

4 House of Lords, Session 1987–8, 4th Report, *Financing the Community*, p. 16, q. 49.

5 J. Delors (1988) 'L'Europe en mouvement' in *1992, et après ...*, *L'événement européen: initiatives et débats*, no. 3/4 (Seuil).

6 *Agence Europe*, 23 March 1989, p. 13.

7 COM(88)703 final.

Chapter 6

1 For the first, see D. Marquand (1989), *Faltering Leviathan: National Sovereignty, the Regions and Europe*, Report prepared for the Wyndham Place Trust and for the second, K. Dyson, (1980), *The State Tradition in Western Europe* (Oxford, Martin Robertson).

100

2   The discussion which follows is strongly influenced by the Padoa-Schioppa report (1987) *Efficiency, stability and equity: a strategy for the evolution of the economic system of the European Community*, Report of a Study Group appointed by the Commission of the European Communities (Oxford University Press), especially Chapter 13, 'The Community budget and the redistribution function'.

3   COM(87)101, p. 30.

4   T. Padoa-Schioppa, *Efficiency, Stability and Equity*, p. 141.

5   OJ C 194 of 28 July 1982, p. 3.

6   P. Ludlow (1989), *Beyond 1992: Europe and its Western Partners*, Centre for European Policy Studies, Paper No. 38, p. 26.

7   Council Regulation No. 1969/88 of 24 June 1988.

8   *Financial Times*, 28 October 1987.

9   Commission of the European Communities (1978), *Financing the Community Budget: The Way Ahead*, Bulletin, Supplement 8/78, p. 15.

10   The phrase was used by Helen Wallace in her evidence to the House of Lords Select Committee on the European Communities in its report on the Community Budget 1986–7 (HL 239), p. 34.

11   Centre for European Policy Studies, *The Future of Community Finance*, p. 52.

12   COM(87)101, p. 25.

Related titles

Europe's Domestic Market
Jacques Pelkmans and L. Alan Winters
with Helen Wallace

As the nations of the European Community approach the 1992 deadline for the full integration of Europe's internal market, this paper provides a critical analysis of that objective. It discusses the kind of common market which might be achieved and the economic benefits which might follow. But the authors also explore how far other economic measures need to be undertaken, and the other conditions which may need to be satisfied, if governments, industries and public opinion are to endorse the steps necessary to make the European economy more dynamic. They end with an optimistic assessment of the future of the British economy in a unified European market.

Forthcoming

The Future of European Competition Policy
edited by Peter Montagnon

This paper looks at the kind of competition policy that Europe needs for the single European market of the 1990s. It covers merger control, European competition policy and national utilities, state subsidy programmes and the impact of competition policy on commercial policy. There are contributions from Heinrich Hoelzler (German Confederation of Industry), Joseph Gilchrist and John Deakin (European Commission) and Dieter Helms (Oxford University). Two underlying questions are addressed: what policies should Europe pursue in the 1990s, and what respective roles will national and Community authorities play in implementing these policies?

Making a Reality of the Single European Market
Michael Hodges and Stephen Woolcock

This paper compares the British and German responses to the single European market. It considers how companies and public policy-makers are responding to the challenges represented by 1992 and how these interact. It includes case-studies in mergers and acquisitions, public procurement, standards, telecommunications and financial services. The book, which is based on research carried out in Britain and Germany with the Institut für Europäische Politik in Bonn, contrasts the deregulatory approach of the British with the more consensus-based approach of the Federal Republic of Germany and discusses the implications of these alternative approaches for the future shape of the single market.

RIIA/PINTER PUBLISHERS